Financial Meltdown in the Mainline?

Loren B. Mead

An Alban Institute Publication

Library of Congress Catalog Number 97-78127
ISBN 1-56699-197-8

DEDICATION

To

Elizabeth Courtney Wise
James Benjamin Stallworth Wise
Loren Benjamin Mead, II
Nicholas Alexander Mead

participant leaders for the church of the future

CONTENTS

FOREWORD

My dictionary advises that a foreword is supposed to be an introductory remark or prefatory note about a piece of writing. Its purpose is to propel a reader into a book, to set the stage for an exchange of ideas, to make room for a precious human activity: thinking.

That is exactly what I want to do for Loren Mead's latest book, *Financial Meltdown in the Mainline?* I want to invite you to become part of a conversation that will at times make you uncomfortable. At least it should. I want to encourage readers to stay with a book that they may be tempted to put down. Those responses will arise in part because this book probes an especially sensitive area in our lives and our religious institutions—the troubled relationship between faith and money. But they may also occur because of the author's style. This is a book that uses strong language, one that sets out to provoke a reaction. Expect to be challenged here by words that speak unsparingly about our personal and collective denial of the financial realities confronting us. Get ready to ponder a diagnosis of a pervasive addiction to money that afflicts us all.

Those familiar with the Alban Institute will not be surprised by this book's style. Those who know Loren Mead, who have heard him lecture or been privileged to sit in more informal conversations with him, will be able to hear his voice rise and fall on these pages. His South Carolina cadences and his folksy ways of making very large points are present on every page. Many will respond to this book by saying that it is "typically Loren."

It is, but for more reasons than his transparent writing style. This book is typically Loren and typically Alban because it is about a very real, and very difficult, problem at the heart of American congregational and denominational life. Money. The pages that follow will tell you that most of our churches and synagogues don't have enough of it. What we do have, we don't manage very well. As individuals and as leaders of institutions, we don't tell the truth about the power of money in our lives. We don't even know how to think and talk well about this issue.

From the time of its founding, the Alban Institute has devoted itself to helping clergy, congregation members, denominational leaders and others concerned about the health of our religious institutions take on just such tough problems. So it should come as no surprise that the Institute would publish this book and that Alban's founder would be its author. For almost a quarter of a century that kind of engagement with the issues that tie our congregations up in knots, the obstacles that impede or block ministry, the threats to our institutional and personal existence, has been Alban's hallmark.

This book is typical of Loren Mead and of Alban in another sense. It is a product of the author's more than forty years of action-reflection, a distinct way of learning. It is an outcome of a career-long journey through the institutional netherworld of American religion. Throughout that journey, but especially in the years since he retired from the Institute's presidency and returned his full energies to his first love, consulting, Mead has watched as congregations, clergy, denominational leaders, and other concerned religious citizens came to terms—or, more often, failed to—with economic reality. He has talked with people caught in the crises of shortfalls, windfalls, embezzlements, and poor planning. As he has worked with people in trouble to find solutions, he has gathered an enormous amount of data and practical wisdom about our situation. These years of acting and thinking have led Mead to some deeply held convictions that can become starting points for our own reflection.

A good starting point for reflection is the book's title. "Financial meltdown" is a provocative, evocative image. Mead chose it deliberately, to seize our attention, to shock us into recognition. As we read along with him, we must grapple with that image which condenses a lifetime of experience and a whole set of convictions. Mead believes we are in much more serious financial trouble than we are willing to admit. The situation is so dangerous, he perceives, that this gracious, friendly Episcopal priest finds himself taking on an uncomfortable role. He invokes the great prophet Jeremiah who walked the streets of Jerusalem wearing a yoke of slavery in a desperate attempt to call his people to their senses. Instead of that agricultural gesture of ancient times, Mead opts for one from high technology: Chernobyl—nuclear disaster. Like Jeremiah, Mead intends to carry that extreme reminder into our daily reality to jolt us. Like Jeremiah, Mead agonizes over his message and hopes that it may prove wrong.

But Mead has significant evidence on his side. Declining membership statistics. Shrinking percentages of disposable personal income going to churches and synagogues. Ever more congregations slipping beneath the viability line—at least for the prevailing full-service model of parish ministry. Downsizing. Budget creep. Deferred maintenance and naive fiscal practices. Ecclesiastical doublespeak that allows leaders to describe losses as gains. A huge ecclesiastical entitlement system. Misappropriation of funds. Rising litigation costs. An aging donor pool and the lack of readiness on the part of a new generation to step forward and provide support. The list goes on. Those who choose to reject his meltdown image must do so in the face of very serious realities.

There is a still deeper reason for Mead's choice of metaphors. Beneath all the economic indicators is another fundamental reality. Financial meltdown is only a symptom of a deeper crisis. At one point he asks, "What is going on in our hearts that has let us get so deeply in trouble, and what has kept us from doing something about it long before now?" (page 82)   In classic prophetic style, Mead is identifying a spiritual crisis. We have, he claims, failed to connect the worldly reality of money with the spiritual realities of sin and grace. Ironically, here is one of the leading organizational consultants in American religion, often sought out for "quick fixes" and new institutional techniques, calling for repentance and urging on us a new, sacramental way of viewing money.

"Just as bread and wine can become life-giving pointers to more than bread and wine, I assert at the end of this book that our budgets and our organizational systems are pointers to reality beyond ourselves." (page 6)   I hear his call for repentance echoing centuries of battles in both Judaism and Christianity between those who see all of life as God's arena—a seamless spiritual reality—and those who for various secular and sacred reasons wish to separate the things of this world from those of the spirit.

It is time to propel you into this book. There is much to ponder here. Engage Mead in addressing a variety of questions and issues of great importance—on which you may or may not agree. Start with the large questions: Are we in a time of meltdown or not? What about the deeper spiritual crisis described here? But also spend time on more particular questions such as whether clergy do fail to address the money issue. Is that true? Why is it so hard for clergy to talk with people about money? What can we do about the ecclesiastical entitlement system? There are many more such compelling questions awaiting you.

These questions emerge alongside several energizing suggestions for assuring that Mead's meltdown metaphor does not become reality. Mead has wonderful ideas about an invigorated leadership role for the older generation of congregation members. He also suggests new ways of helping people talk together about this vital issue in their lives. Mead's hope is that a new, honest, biblical engagement with the world of money may open important new avenues of ministry. I join him in urging you to find them.

James P. Wind
President, The Alban Institute

ACKNOWLEDGMENTS

This book represents my decades of following a trail of learning from leaders and participants in religious congregations. As such, it represents the best knowledge I was able to pick up, deduce, discover, or gather in hundreds of conferences, books, periodicals, agency reports—in short, wherever I could dig it up.

I came to the issue of churches and money reluctantly. But as I followed the trail of the past forty years, the issue just kept coming up. I tried to focus on organizational issues to explain the difficult situation religious institutions are in at the end of the twentieth century (the material I dealt with in *The Once and Future Church*), and I ran across issues of money. I tried to point ahead of today's institutions to the forms we will need in the twenty-first century (the material I dealt with in *Transforming Congregations for the Future*), and I ran across the issue of money more frequently. Then I tried to outline the obstacles the churches face in making it into the future (the material I dealt with in *Five Challenges to the Once and Future Church*), and again money kept coming up.

I wrote this book because I couldn't avoid the task if I wanted to pass along what I have learned that may help the next generation of religious leaders.

Because this material came in drips and drabs from here and there, it probably is not as coherent as I might hope. Much of it takes off from data I have discovered and have interpreted in ways that the gatherers of the data probably did not expect. My problem was my own growing conviction that money not only is the Achilles heel of the religious institutional forms we have, but it is also a subject that religious leaders on the whole avoid like the plague. I have not solved either of those problems, but I hope I have made them more accessible to the next generation of leaders.

I must thank many people who have passed me bits of information, copies of denominational reports, or just hunches. I must thank the journalists of the churches and of the secular press who try to tell the truth to a skeptical audience in the churches. I must thank the few who have begun to do research on different dimensions of the issue; I try to note many of their contributions specifically in footnotes. I must also thank the leaders of the Lilly Endowment, Inc., who have begun funding a number of projects that are already beginning to throw light on this subject. I specifically thank Craig Dykstra and Fred Hofheinz, who encouraged my work in this area.

In the text I note the contributions of Robert Wood Lynn to scholarship about the history of financial support of churches in this country. I must state that his friendship and support through this project have been terribly important. When I was at my most perplexed, wondering if I were crazy because nobody seemed to agree with me about how important it was, Bob Lynn's off-the-cuff comment in an article I was reading made me know there were at least two crazy people in the world. And I guess I would rather be crazy with Bob Lynn than sane with most others! His continuing critique and comment have meant the world.

A word of appreciation to my cruel, slave-driving supervisor, Douglass Lewis of Wesley Seminary. Doug's practical assistance, coming as it did from one of the ones most directly involved in practical financial and development work for theological education, helped me see dimensions of the problem I had not seen before. He has enormous gifts in development that I hope to see more widely used in the churches. An unintended, but enormously graceful, part of his supervisory relationship was the opportunity to share in the marriage ceremony of his daughter, Laura, and my son, Christopher.

One final group served as my tutors in this subject—the pastors and leaders of congregations with endowments. Nearly two decades ago I ran into some of those congregations, many as reluctant to face the financial dimension of the churches as I was. Somehow, as we worked together, we began to see how the financial issues opened up to very large issues of law and grace. I consider my work with the networks of Episcopal and Presbyterian Churches to have been one of my best venues for learning. Our inability to launch similar networks in other denominations has been a disappointment to me—one that I hope to work on in the next few years.

In former days authors acknowledged all kinds of technical support from friends and co-workers. I must claim most of the technical support came from the invisible and mysterious internal workings of my Power-Book. Thank you, therefore, Stephen Jobs. One of the things I learned about stepping down from institutional leadership is that one does not lose any work, but one loses one's secretary!

And my wife, Polly, has been marvelous. She puts up with my grim face after hours of seemingly fruitless effort. Now that she has banished me to the basement for my writing, our relationship has become much more creative. When I come up for air, she can sense immediately if the necessary prescription is to see friends, to go to a movie, or a more liquid tonic.

So, friends, here it is. I hope it helps you make sense of what is going on where you are. There are gaps in what I know, but I've tried to note them. There are areas I can only point to as problems, because I haven't a clue what we can do about them. But I give this flawed piece to you as another of my notes from the field, trusting you to take it further.

Loren B. Mead

CHAPTER 1

Why the "Nuclear" Alarm?

Financial meltdown may be underway in the mainline churches of this country. And I suspect that other Christian denominations are a few steps behind the mainline.[1]

Meltdown is a strong word, which carries potent emotional images. It calls to mind the nuclear crisis at Chernobyl in the Ukraine. In April 1986 radioactive fall-out in Scandinavia was traced back to the Ukraine. I remember the horror when the news of the Chernobyl disaster first hit. Something was dreadfully wrong, but no one knew quite what was happening. Reports did surface of extraordinarily brave people battling to contain the damage, many of them sacrificing their very lives. Today the land and people of the Ukraine are still suffering from that disaster.

Closer to home, the word brings to mind images of the earlier Three Mile Island crisis and frightened Pennsylvanians east of Harrisburg fleeing their homes, uncertain about what sort of catastrophe they faced. There, too, quick, sacrificial actions prevented a cataclysmic disaster.

As threatening and damaging as these incidents were, note that in neither horrific case did meltdown actually occur. The word refers to a more terrible reality, which, thank God, has never occurred—yet. "Yet" gives one pause! In a true meltdown, what began to happen both at Chernobyl and Three Mile Island is carried to its conclusion. A catastrophic set of events rapidly careens out of control: Nuclear fuel heats beyond its safety limits; the heat controls break down; all controls collapse and the nuclear mass generates unmanageable, explosive heat. In true meltdown, the entire mass becomes molten; the containers melt, then the underlying concrete, the very earth itself, and an apocalyptic, unknowable event happens, possibly the kind of earth-disrupting explosion that could lead to the extinction of all life for miles around and for thousands of years. When true meltdown gets under way, no human action can stop it.

There is no guarantee that nuclear meltdown will not occur at some time in the future. And every human being, every animal, and every tree has a strong stake in the effectiveness of every engineer in every nuclear power plant anywhere in the world. Without them, meltdown could occur at any time in any such plant.

I use the word *meltdown* knowing that it is strong language. When I do so in terms of our religious institutions, I am mindful of the story of the prophet Jeremiah, who tried to tell his friends in Jerusalem that their foreign policy was leading them to Babylonian enslavement. When people would not pay attention, he strengthened his metaphor. He walked the streets wearing a yoke on his shoulders. Friends said he was wrong, broke the yoke, and sent him on his way. He pondered what they had said, then got another yoke and went back on the streets.

I know it is presumptuous, even arrogant, of me to identify with what he did, and yet Jeremiah's story prompts me to continue to use inflammatory language. Jeremiah hoped he was wrong and that the situation would change. So do I. Jeremiah tried to rethink his message when others challenged him, but even so he did not change it. Neither can I, although I would give an arm if I could!

Why am I compelled to use the meltdown image?

Our Crisis May Be Irreversible

I sense an irreversible nature to what has begun to happen within the finances of the religious institutions I have worked with for half a century—institutions that have nurtured me, institutions I love.

My concern is not fueled by nostalgia for the churches of the past century. Although those forms of church have nurtured my life, I have no desire to preserve those forms as I remember them. The catastrophic loss I foresee is not some kind of desire to turn back the clock. What I am articulating is substantially different from the misty-eyed nostalgia of religion aficionados who deplore the loss of the religiosity Americans have grown used to. There are those who deplore the disappearance of Victorian morals and spirituality, who yearn for the days when "all the young people dressed well, came to church, and obeyed their elders."

They believe that some amalgam of romanticism and fervor can put God back on his male throne in heaven where he "ought" to be. Let me be clear: I have no stake in preserving some kind of church that Westerners generally have confused with the cultural status quo of the first half of the twentieth century. Good riddance to much of that, as far as I am concerned. When I talk about meltdown, I am warning against the disastrous loss of a different dimension altogether.

Full-fledged meltdown would mean the collapse of the infrastructure that has carried Christianity into the homes, values, lives of people across this continent. It would mean the vaporization of the life of the congregations in which millions of us worship every Sunday and from which we are baptized, married, and buried. It would begin with the breakdown of the structures and links by which church people in one place work with and support believers in other places. It would lead to the loss of most educational institutions dedicated to training religious and ethical leaders for society. It would make museums and music centers of the great places of worship that do survive. In a generation or two, the voice of the religious conscience in the public arena would be stilled; works of loving care would no longer be focused on issues distant from one's own doorstep. Faith connection and support would become happenstance, and prophets would stand alone—if they stand at all. Every characteristic of the church that has made it reach into society and nurture new generations in faith would cease to exist.[2]

I have shared some of the thinking in this book with friends and colleagues. Almost universally they urge me to stay away from the word *meltdown,* because it is too strong. They agree with the data I present— such as those in the chapters that follow—but they say, "You overstate the ramifications," or, "Yes, there are difficulties out there, but give us time. We are working on them." Then there are those who say, "That may be true of other places or other churches, but it is different here where I am."

Tempered by my colleagues, I say that I *trust* we are still in the early stages of disaster, as at Chernobyl and Three Mile Island, where the fullness of a final meltdown can be averted. Both Chernobyl and Three Mile Island were contained before the unstoppable chain of events started "firing." The ultimate explosion, meltdown, did not occur, because of the heroic action of people at the scene. Note the significant difference between what happened at Chernobyl and at Three Mile Island.

In the Ukraine an unknown number died then or are dying now as a result of what happened. Farm land will lie fallow for centuries before it can again grow safe crops. Costs were astronomical, and they are not over yet. The Pennsylvania accident produced far less long-term damage. And the human factor made the difference—the level of engineering, the emergency command structure, the training and expertise of plant workers—all were significantly stronger in Pennsylvania. I hope the implication of this for the churches is clear: that our skills and insights and our quick response can make a difference in the outcome of the crisis into which we are heading.

Neither of those nuclear crises was solved by committee meetings and reorganizations. Neither crisis was contained by "business as usual," or "next year's strategic planning." Neither crisis containment began until individual people acted, recognizing that it was time for substantial, heroic effort. Again, I hope that the churches still have time to act before disaster is irreversible.

I am writing this book because I believe that how we respond to our crisis will make a difference for the church of tomorrow.

Wake Up Now!

I use the inflammatory language for another reason. I believe it is time for a wake-up call to ourselves and our church leadership. Our religious institutions are vitally important for carrying religious traditions and values to future generations. The next centuries and millennia will desperately need what has been conveyed to us through the traditions of our faith communities in our congregations, synagogues, parishes, and communities. But I do not believe those remarkable institutions will make it through the next two generations without the kind of dedication, commitment, and sacrifice that addressed the crises in Chernobyl and Pennsylvania. I believe that the quality of leadership response will make a difference.

So far, I am disappointed in what I have seen in the churches' response to the crisis I will describe in later chapters. I see strategic planning processes, rarely with any sense of urgency. I see restructuring, downsizing, and renewal projects. I see endless New Initiatives, Mission Imperatives, Plans for the Next Millennium.

But I don't see people going to the roots, trying to address the radical nature of the change that will take more courage than we have been willing to dredge up. I hear little straight talk.

Crisis at the Core

I use strong language to describe the crisis, because the financial meltdown issue is pointed straight at deeper, more central questions of meaning for our world and for the vocation of the churches within this world. It is much more than budgets and finances. It involves even more than rebuilding denominational structures.

Why is it that churches—with all their faults, made up of remarkable people, many seeking diligently to make the world a better place as well as to become better people themselves—seem to do such an inadequate job of keeping their own house in order in terms of finances? How could they have let their financial situation reach a point that it could even be considered a meltdown?

Why, in a society that is so wealthy and money conscious, are churches unable to be even modestly effective in managing their own financial condition? Why are they unable even to identify or clarify what is happening? What is there in the way they operate or see themselves that makes them sound uncertain trumpets in this area so central to their members and their world?

As I consider those questions, I realize that I do not think that the financial meltdown condition is really a matter of mathematical incompetence or organizational ignorance. If it were, the solution would be simple education in accounting and bookkeeping and organizational leadership training. You can learn to be competent mathematically or organizationally.

The problem is not at the accidental level of how we organize or pay our bills, how we structure ourselves and follow up our mission objectives. It is about the central religious question of our time: Do we live in a world circumscribed entirely by what we see and touch, or is everything we see and touch part of a related system grounded in God? It is also about the central spiritual questions each of us faces daily: Are we personally responsible for the things and relationships in which we live, or is life a charade with the prize going to anybody who collects the most toys? Are we cared about and called to be caring? Or is it all an enormous joke played on us by the universe? Do things have value? Do we have value? Are we "just here," or are we called to be here?

These important questions are central to our human experience. And these questions and how we answer them are critical dimensions in our struggle to divert disaster in our recalcitrant organizational systems and looming budget problems. I believe that the threat of financial meltdown is a great invitation to religious leaders not only to work at solving financial problems, but perhaps for the first time to engage the issues of value and choice through which every human being is struggling to work out his or her salvation—with fear and trembling.[3]

Let me say it in more traditional terms, at least in my own tradition. Many readers will know I am an Episcopalian. Not an uncritical Episcopalian, yet a committed one. I have a love-hate relationship with my church, and most of the time it's love. I speak out of the special tradition that's mine, because it's the language I know. I trust you to "translate" the words I use to meanings that fit your tradition. We Episcopalians, like many others, make a lot of the fact that in the Eucharist we meet Christ. Some generations and traditions have fought wars over what that simple statement meant—trying to define where and how Christ is "in" the Eucharist. That's not my kind of issue, but I don't put down those debates or the importance of them. I'm just not interested in fighting that war. What I know is that from a lifetime of experience, I find that I can count on Christ's being there when we do what he told us to do on the night of his betrayal. I don't always "feel" or "experience" him. It often "happens" for me without my fully understanding it. The bread and the wine are important ingredients in that meeting. The other things are important, too—the place, the people I'm with, the familiar words and actions. The experience of his presence really does come to me in what my tradition calls Eucharist. The spiritual experience somehow comes in dialogue with the things and actions, with the bread and the wine.

Just as bread and wine can become life-giving pointers to more than bread and wine, I assert at the end of this book that our budgets and our organizational systems are pointers to reality beyond themselves. I believe they are doorways through which we can address some of the spiritual dilemmas of our own lives and our society. As we in the churches face the threat of financial meltdown, we must address real spiritual meltdowns that are going on in our society and our times.

For most of this book, I will be dealing with the issues of dollars and budgets, of organizations and reorganizations. Of course I do not write with pure objectivity. I care about these things. I do not write entirely on the basis of empirical data, but on the basis of far-ranging conversations with dozens of wise church leaders in many denominations and on the basis of wide reading in the churches' publications, especially regional ones. More of my learning has come in consulting with groups within church bodies and agencies—local, regional, and national. Data lie behind what I say, and I will share much of them. But I am well aware that I am also speaking from experience and instinct—honed through a half century of caring about the churches, working with them, trying to understand them and help them be more faithful and effective.

My point of view, however, is that these specific, empirical issues of organization and finance are clues to and doors into the heart of the church's calling and work. It is not enough simply to solve the financial and organizational problems, so we can "fix" the mess we are in. Rather, in working on the financial mess we have allowed ourselves to get in, we have a chance to touch the heart of some of the *spiritual meltdown* that may also be happening around us.

In short, the financial meltdown is a wake-up call for us not to "fix the church," but to be about our Father's business.

CHAPTER 2

What's Visible to the Naked Eye

In this chapter I present visible problematic issues on the church scene. To this picture I want to add what I foresee out ahead because of these issues, and why I see these issues as signs that we may be approaching something much more serious—what I am calling meltdown. Accurate information about financial matters in the churches is difficult to locate for any number of reasons. For starters, each denomination operates as a universe in and of itself. That is further complicated by the fact that congregations within a denomination often operate individualistic information systems barely compatible with the systems of their own denomination. To say nothing of the fact that some groups within the churches hide information—especially financial information—from others.

An obvious obstacle to analysis is the different categorizations of funds. What does the congregational budget category "mission expenses" mean? In some cases it means the costs of starting a new congregation nearby. In some cases it means support that goes to a denominational effort overseas, including judicatory and/or denominational administrative salaries. Or it can refer to any funds sent anywhere outside the congregation. Or to a special commitment a particular congregation has made to a project close at hand (a food bank) or far away (a particular evangelistic effort in New Guinea). What one Presbyterian congregation identifies as "mission expense" may be quite different from what another, just a few miles away, calls mission.

An important study by Dean Hoge, Jackson Carroll, and Francis Scheets made this point forcefully.[1] Within four denominations they tried to determine how much it cost a congregation to support a full-time pastor. Printed budgets and denominational reports helped little. Categories such as "parsonage," "transportation," and "utilities" meant something different in each congregation.

One who is trying to understand how a congregation uses its resources is going to have a difficult time. Church boards and agencies add to the confusion by changing categories every few years, so that a budget from one year does not quite fit the budget used the next year—or at least several years later. This makes it hard to get long-range data. In my experience congregational data from even the immediate past year are often hard to locate, and it is almost hopeless to seek data from a decade earlier. If data are available at all, the change in categories has made comparing the information impossible. I rarely see data comparisons except in the most sophisticated congregations, where changes related to cost of living or inflation are only occasionally acknowledged.

Most churches with which I work that are planning for the "long range" rely on information from only the past three or four years. What is true of congregations is doubly true for regional and national church bodies. Often data are available only for the time during which the current pastor (or executive or bishop) has had leadership. Because long-term trends are not known, the short-term data are often used primarily to justify or attack a current leader in comparison to the former incumbent!

Another factor complicates the communication of clear data in religious circles. Churches do not often understand or deal with what inflation does to their dollars. Congregations tell me that they have moved from a budget of $180,000 a year to $240,000 in only ten years. They say so with great pride in the accomplishment. Few seem able to face the reality that such a congregation, all things considered, is worse off today than it was a decade ago, when one factors in the increased cost of routine expenditures. If one uses the low-inflation years from 1982-92, it would take $271,452 in 1992 to have the purchasing power of $180,000 ten years earlier. I find this confusing, knowing that many people on the boards of those congregations manage businesses that routinely take such change into account.[2] One cannot help wondering about such unthinking behavior by competent people who are committed to their churches.

I am not trying to make a case for "absolute perfection" in the accounting systems in the churches; I am pointing out that the hodgepodge system we have makes it difficult to know what is actually going on. If one is able to discover what is going on in the present, it is virtually impossible to make comparisons with statistics of ten years ago. The fact that each denomination has its own system adds to the complication if one tries to get a larger, more comprehensive picture of the financial condition of the churches.

If one were naturally suspicious, one might conclude that the systems were allowed to be as confusing as they are to keep us from knowing something. Or facing something. I do not believe the reporting systems are intentionally misleading, but I am certain that the way we use them in actual practice hides more information than it provides. One wonders why.

Secondary Indicators

Because of the problem in ferreting out reliable and comparable numbers about congregational and denominational finances, I propose we look at some secondary indicators.

Restructuring and Downsizing

In many cases restructuring and downsizing at denominational national or regional offices or church agencies are two indicators of a financial crisis. Sometimes the news appears "in small print"—the "retirement" of an agency staff member with news of the elimination of programs that person managed. Sometimes major national-office downsizing is announced as a new initiative in mission.[3] Presbyterians have come to expect announcements of restructuring of some sort almost every year, with Episcopalians usually experiencing slightly longer periods between downsizings. United Methodist restructuring is not as easy to observe, because the denomination's national staff is separated into quasi-independent boards. The current plans for a major downsizing in the national staff structures of the Southern Baptist Sunday School Board are exacerbated by the growing split between the conservative and the more moderate wings of that community of churches. In the major denominations, regional restructuring also occurs frequently.

Nearly twenty years ago I ran across a small book by two angry pioneers, Robert Wilson and Paul Mickey.[4] They were angry, because as national church bureaucrats they did not like what was happening to the mission and the mission staff of their own denomination, the United

Methodist Church. They were pioneers, because they asked around and found out that what was happening in their denomination was also happening to colleagues in a number of other denominational headquarters in New York. The book is as current today as it was when it was written. Not much has changed in how the denominations and their bureaucracies interact with one another. They still call it the same thing, "restructuring"; they do it without regard to what happened in their last restructuring; and they do it as if restructuring in other denominations is irrelevant to them.

As I reread their small book today, I am impressed with one clear truth: What people were talking about and arguing about—the arguments for this kind of organization or that, the effort to keep one kind of staff on board and let go of another—all of these conversations missed the point.

They had run out of money. They couldn't support the staff they had. The budgetary shortfall made it imperative for changes to be made. Those changes were made—some with sensitivity, some not.

Wilson and Mickey pointed out that what was happening in one denomination was happening in many. There was a kind of interdenominational crisis going on, but everyone was paying attention only to one's own denomination's experience. And even to one's own compartment in one's own denomination.

I noted another remarkable thing: The arguments about the restructuring—what was being restructured, who was being squeezed out or up, why such action was being taken—rarely dealt with the underlying financial shortfall. People blamed people; people preached jeremiads against the "others"; people decried liberalism or conservatism or one or another kind of theology; but rarely did they look squarely at the financial problem and try to do anything about that.

The rhetoric about the proposed changes tended to suggest that after a long period of wandering in the wilderness, current leaders of the agency (or denomination, seminary, or whatever) were now, finally, structuring themselves to give brutally effective leadership to bring the people into the promised land. The assumption that all past leaders had been irresponsible was never baldly stated, but many of the old leaders I knew personally were deeply hurt by the implications. Wilson and Mickey pointed out that all the trouble signs they saw then at the end of the sixties suggested that the storm of restructuring was just beginning. But each denomination's leaders assumed that they had fixed the leak in their own boat.

An organizational fundamentalism gripped the denominations: Whatever is wrong, we can fix it if we "restructure." I have seen a lot of restructuring in church systems over the past twenty or thirty years (the first one I remember occurred about 1968 in my own denomination), but I have never seen any credible evidence that a restructured organization really did things substantially better than its predecessor. I am at a loss to understand how such an uncertain tool became subject of such unquestioning acceptance.

Because I read many church periodicals, I keep abreast of news in many denominations. Because I remember the lessons of Wilson and Mickey, I read such institutional news with a questioning eye. I particularly mark what I call sequential restructuring, by which I mean patterns of periodic downsizing. Few of the denominations with which I am familiar have avoided this pattern. So whenever I hear about restructuring, my ears prick up. Almost always, if I look hard enough, I discover that they ran short of money. But the rhetoric rarely mentions the financial roots of the problem, except in passing.

My point is not that each of these is necessarily a crisis, but that the pattern is pervasive enough to be disquieting. If even a few of the stories of restructuring are driven by shortfalls of financial support, we are dealing with a widespread phenomenon within the religious world, a phenomenon with very great implications for the future of the organizational structures the denominations count on. Our exclusive focus on the surface issue—the restructuring—makes us blind to the financial roots of the problem.

Controversy

Just as I have come to look below the surface whenever I see the words *restructure* or *downsizing* in a news report, I do the same when I note the word *controversy*. My colleagues and I at the Alban Institute are "on call" to assist in conflicts and controversies. This means that in my reading of church periodicals, I pay attention when I see signs of a church fight. About two years ago I picked up signals that a fight was brewing in Richmond, Virginia, in an institution I have come to regard highly, the

Presbyterian School of Christian Education. The alumni were up in arms about the board's plans to sell a dormitory to Baptists who were starting a theological seminary in town. Some of the argument had to do with the love the alumni had for the building. Some sounded like a theological problem of collaborating with the (horror of horrors) Southern Baptists. Some alumni were demanding to be consulted. Others were pleading for school expansion. Other interested parties were raising questions about the future of PSCE. In the news article I read of the controversy, I saw little discussion of what I sense was the real issue, money. Though I do not know for sure, I suspect that the board did not have the money to bring the building up to date, the building was unnecessary for the size of the student body, and, besides all that, the income from the sale would be most helpful in balancing the budget or reducing indebtedness. These were my guesses, because little information came out in the public about the money issue. The public discussion of the controversy was about ideas and commitments, about hopes and memories.[5] I believe my guesses were right, now that the PSCE and Union (Presbyterian) Seminary of Richmond have announced a merger.

Another controversy I ran across occurred in New Mexico in the Catholic Church. Here the issue was the sale of a beloved retreat center, the Dominican Retreat House. As reported, "Tens of thousands of people have been through the retreat house since its founding thirty-seven years ago. Themes of its low cost retreats range from the Catholic mystical tradition to counseling for alcoholism." The loyal constituents were fighting the sale. A board member was quoted, "We are poor people here who can't afford to go to expensive retreat centers. . . . What are we going to do?" But the archdiocese was feeling other pressures—costs of litigation. The report says that twelve pieces of property were to be sold to cover costs.[6] That's some financial bind! Although I did not see stories of those other eleven situations, I would be willing to bet there was controversy in many of them, though the issue of the financial problem may well have been similarly avoided.

The *New York Times* gave me another controversy to consider. The headline read "A Church in Crisis Over Arts."[7] This fascinating feature on a fight at the Episcopal Church of Saint Ann and the Holy Trinity dealt with very complex relationships between a local parish and a neighboring center for the arts. The fight led to charges of racism, poor administration, misunderstandings, and misuse of resources. The problem? People on the two sides did not agree on facts or interpretations, but it seemed the church building was about to collapse, and it seemed that the money raised for the church restoration had been funneled into the arts center.

As I see it, the bottom line in a church fight such as this that hits the newspaper headlines is that a financial collapse has occurred. The fight, whatever it really was about, began with a financial shortfall. The public hears about the battle between those who support art and those who support religious services. They hear about what sounds like power grabbing shenanigans by people who claim to be Christians, and there is a tinge of glee at hypocrisy exposed. That's what comes out, but the real story is about a shortage of money and poor management of institutional life.

Widespread reorganization and downsizing suggest a financial squeeze occurring across many denominations. Similarly, many reports of church controversies and fights seem to point to pervasive problems with finance. If my hunches are true in only half of the reports that have come to my attention, we have very serious problems.

Other Symptomatic Indicators

Although there are thousands of strong congregations with well-kept plants and able professional staffs supported by broad financial support, some kinds of congregations have a consistently different experience, facing survival issues every year.

The most obvious are the many small congregations with few members and few financial resources, working heroically to maintain at least a minimal institutional viability.[8] This group of congregations is not insubstantial. Over half the congregations in the country have fewer than two hundred members. An interesting unpublished research study by Claude A. Smith gives startling information about the size of local church budgets in the United States, pointing to the fact that the large bulk of congregations in many denominations operate on a budget of less than $100,000.[9] Smith lists the following percentages of congregations below that level:

Total Congregations
Percentage of congregations with budgets less than $100,000

American Baptist Church	5,058	79 %
Disciples of Christ	3,107	62 %
Episcopal	7,413	58 %
Evangelical Lutheran	10,897	60 %
Unitarian Universalist	948	66 %
United Church of Christ[10]	6,137	72 %
United Methodist Church	36,424	78 %

I see these percentages as approximating the percentage of congregations that cannot carry out the minimum program expected by the denomination. Most members of such congregations have to learn to live with the image of dependency or second-class citizenship within their denominational circle. Every year these congregations spend more and more time and effort trying to figure out how to survive as congregations. Creative energy gets sucked into survival, not into figuring out how better to engage in what God calls them to be in that place. Many people in those congregations feel they are falling short of what they are supposed to be.

I explore this issue regularly in workshops, attended by lay leaders, clergy, and executives.[11] I try to find out how these leaders think congregations are getting along financially. This is no precise data collection but an impressionistic exploration of the sense of well-being in the congregations these leaders know. I do this bit of impressionistic research by asking, "How much do you think it takes to 'run' a 'standard' congregation in your part of the world?"

Participants always ask what I mean. "What do you mean by *standard?*" Or, "Is this a church with the mortgage paid up?"

I always do a little dodging, here, so that we don't get into a detailed game but stick with their feelings and intuitions. "Just the usual kind of congregation: one pastor, one building, with enough money to run a little program and make a contribution to the denomination's mission needs. What kind of a budget do you think it takes for a congregation to do that where you live?"

Answers vary widely. Low answers cluster in the $80,000-$110,000 range, but I have heard estimates as low as $50,000 or $60,000. High answers vary from $120,000 on up to more than $200,000.

For my purposes the spread offered at any one workshop is interesting in itself. Participants immediately recognize the wide variety of perceptions among them. We all usually learn a lot from the differences in those perceptions. In each workshop I push the group to agree on what is a "fair" minimum for their part of the country, recognizing that a very fine congregation might be able to "do the job" with significantly less. Groups often can agree on a $90,000 or $100,000 figure as locally characteristic.

With the group having reached a consensus, I bring out the tough question: "Think about the congregations in your denomination in your neighborhood or area." (If I am dealing with bishops or executives, I make it specific: "Think about the congregations under your care.") "What percentage of them do you think have a budget that is below our agreed fair minimum for your area?"

The group's reaction here is dramatic. A gasp, a wow, often even before people start making guesses. So far, in doing this across this country and Canada, every group has felt that at least 40 percent of the congregations they know are operating below what they have defined as the break-even point. Some estimates go as high as 70 or 80 percent.

Again, this is not a scientific sampling. It may, however, be an even better indication for our purposes. This simple question-and-answer exercise makes it clear that many church leaders believe that most congregations currently are not making it financially. They see the local church as an institutional unit that may mean a lot to its members but that in many cases is not able to pay its bills.

The small congregation—whether urban or rural—is very hard put to make it in this economic society. It is under increasingly severe economic pressure. Many of them "make do" the way ingenious people do: They put off fixing the boiler or the roof; they arrange for a long interim between pastors, so they can save up money to support the new one (hoping he or she won't stay *too* long!); they sponsor community fund raisers; they pinch pennies. Some make do on bequests, hoping they can leap from one to another the way a lumberjack crosses a river by jumping from log to log, leaving each just before it goes under water.

Larger congregations also feel economic pressure, even though they have more people contributing to the budget. There's the urgent need for skilled multiple-person staffs to provide specialists for quality programming for a large, diverse constituency. Those staffs are expensive. As are the facilities generally maintained by large congregations. Some large congregations support historic, land-marked building plants that must be maintained despite their dwindling membership. Few of these large congregations have resources for new initiatives or to meet unexpected crises. Even if a large congregation is trying only to maintain the status quo, it frequently faces the budget crunch of income not increasing at the rate of inflation. There are some ways in which very large congregations can provide high-quality programming more efficiently than smaller ones, but the total costs are higher, the burden of inflation is persistent, and making the budget is difficult.

In workshops I often ask people from large congregations this question: "Raise your hand if your congregation made its budget this year fairly easily." Out of several hundred people, fewer than five have raised their hands.

A study conducted in the Episcopal Diocese of Massachusetts attempted to analyze how parish budget size affected how money was spent by congregations. The chart on the following page shows the findings:[12]

Congregations' Operating Costs
(in percentages by congregation size)

	Annual Budget				
	Under $50k	$50k to $99k	$100k to $199k	$200k to $299k	$300k and over
Assessment	6%	5%	8%	11%	11%
Clergy	49%	50%	40%	33%	29%
Worship	8%	7%	8%	8%	8%
Debt Service	1%	1%	3%	2%	0%
Property/ Maintenance	24%	24%	22%	21%	24%
Office	4%	8%	11%	15%	17%
Education	1%	1%	2%	2%	5%
Fellowship	0%	0%	0%	1%	0%
Outreach	2%	2%	3%	4%	3%
Other	5%	1%	3%	3%	3%

Source: Survey date for 85 congregations in the Episcopal Diocese of Massachusetts for 1994 and 1995.

This chart points out how severely constrained large and small congregations are in trying to accomplish mission and carry out program. The very limited resources available for education in any category of congregation, for example, or for outreach, indicate the severe financial constraints at and on the grassroot unit of the denomination.

Small congregations right now demonstrate a real financial survival crisis across the denominations. Large congregations do not all face survival issues, but virtually all know the struggle of balancing budgets when costs continue to go up as fast or faster than income.

The graph shows clearly the constraints on congregations. The smaller congregations have to use almost all resources simply to pay the pastor and the upkeep of the buildings with almost nothing left for education, outreach, or mission. In larger congregations proportionately more is available for those needs, but the pressures are obvious.

Internal Denominational Battles

Another indicator of financial stress in our church systems is in the internal staff competition for the limited available resources. In the past few years in denomination after denomination, I have seen internal fights about program areas as different program staffs battle for survival: the discontinuance (later reversed) of a popular national weekly magazine for pastors; a publishing house being closed in favor of publishing being centered at the denominational headquarters to save money—then subsequent confusion when the savings proved illusory; the successive reductions of subsidies for theological educational institutions; the shifting of money from one mission field to another. A denomination closes its office in Philadelphia. Or a national affairs program in Washington. The closure of beloved institutions—conference centers, schools, children's service agencies—are painful, painful events. In every case these public actions represented decisions to choose one competing need for funds rather than the other. The staffs who love the programs or institutions and lose the budget battle feel hurt and often angry at those whose institutions survive the cuts. Readers of this book can probably add considerably to my list.

Competition for Special Funds

Another symptom of underlying financial stress exists in a new kind of tension I find in denominations as budgets get tighter. When budgets were expanding, people went to that budget income for funding. Now that budgets are declining, a new urgency drives the search for new sources. Wherever there is thought to be a "pot" of money, supplicants cluster like bees around honey. In times of financial stress, money set aside in trust funds, pension funds, building funds, foundations, and endowments seems to be a magnet for all kinds of programmatic tensions, although few of them in the churches have functioned as program funders previously. Many programs "go under" when the funding collapses. But programs with alert, entrepreneurial leaders locate and try to maneuver money from these extra-budgetary funds mentioned above. Sometimes they encounter other administrators looking to feast upon the same pot of money, and a fierce competition breaks out.

In research Dean Hoge and I did about church endowments, one interviewee said with great simplicity, "You know, every church has spenders and savers. Whenever you have an endowment, you're going to find those people fighting each other." Her categories may be over-simplistic, but her analysis of the dynamics rings true. In denominations, the "spenders" tend to be those involved in program; the "savers" tend to be those with fiduciary responsibility for the trusts and pensions. When the budgets of the spenders get pinched, their deep commitment to their programs leads them to where the funds are.

My concern about what the programmatic use of these funds means for the future financial survival of our churches prompts me to urge careful attention to the places where spenders and savers touch. See Appendix A for special concerns I think need to be on the agenda of trustees and managers of church repositories of invested funds in these times of tight budgets and changing financial conditions.

Both trust-fund people and program people are usually deeply committed to the work of their denomination, but they have different responsibilities. Because church leaders make a habit of speaking elliptically and fuzzily about money and are somewhat comfortable with rather loose agreements, they often leave blurred boundary lines between their areas of responsibility. In times when a program is under severe financial threat, these fuzzy boundaries are an invitation to trouble. People who care for trust funds and who love their church dearly are going to have to say no to some of the most beloved programs and church leaders—because it is their responsibility to do so. In times of stress, it is important for them to have clear guidelines to help them make decisions.

My point is that many of these conversations can escalate into adversarial procedures, simply because they touch sensitivities and deep commitments. We need to begin to recognize that in times of financial stress and shortage, tension is going to be the normal thing. To prepare for those tensions rather than to use each as a battleground seems to me to be the better way.

On the other hand, the presence of those tensions is an indicator of the pressures I have been describing as a possible sign of meltdown.

Other Disturbing Information

In two areas—membership trends and church member giving patterns—
we are beginning to see long-term data that have very significant implications for the future financial condition of religious bodies.

Membership Trends

Membership information is published annually in the *Yearbook of
American and Canadian Churches*.[13] Recognizing that each denomination reports according to its own guidelines and that "membership" often
has distinct and differing definitions among denominations (or, indeed,
sometimes even within a denomination), the curve of membership reported over the past fifty years in the United States tends to follow a
similar pattern, with significant differences from denomination to
denomination.

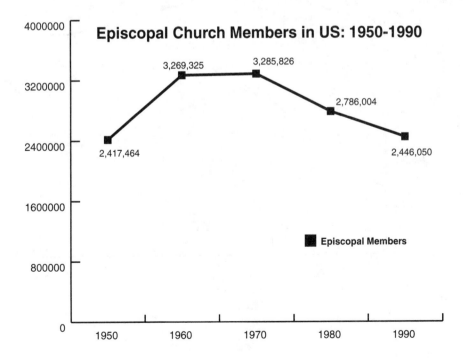

Here is the curve for my own denomination, the Episcopal Church, which demonstrates the pattern among denominations that have had significant membership losses in recent decades. This curve shows a significantly increased membership right after the Second World War; this was a "baby boom" era in which people moved to suburbs; families went to church together. The curve flattens out in the sixties, beginning to decline in the latter half of the sixties, and continues to do so into the nineties.

A number of other denominations have a similar curve. The curves of the Evangelical Lutheran Church in America and United Methodist Church are a bit flatter because of their overall size. The Presbyterian Church (USA) and United Church of Christ have more precipitous declines. Here are graphs of the same data for the United Methodist Church and the Presbyterian Church (USA):

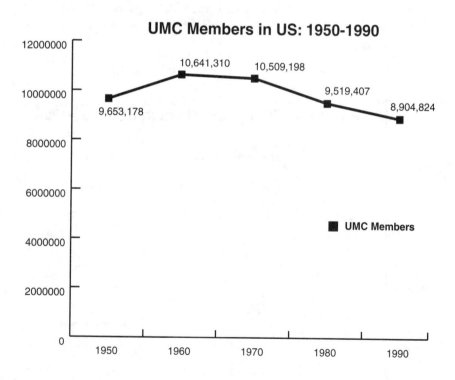

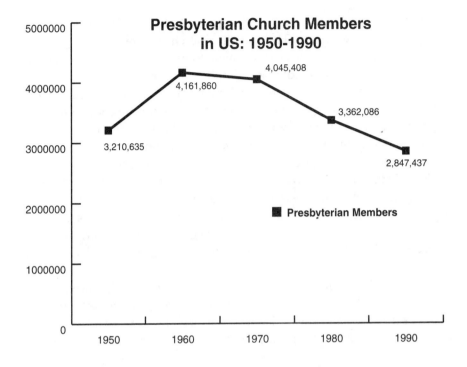

There are denominations —not among those considered "mainline"— whose post-World War II growth continued into the seventies. Many of them indicate a flattening out in the eighties and nineties.

Theories and passions abound in interpreting the data, and I am aware how much my own judgment in this matter is shaped by my opinions, values, and hunches. Almost as long as analysts have been looking at membership data, there has been a significant debate going on, most recently stated by Roger Finke and Rodney Stark.[14] There is clear emotional involvement by researchers and church members in denominations perceived to be "winners" and "losers." And there is a strong pattern of internal denominational scapegoating wherever declines become known. Passions run high around the numbers game.

What can we know for sure in this area? Most denominations did have extraordinary growth during the forties and fifties; most have experienced some flattening out after that rapid increase; and currently a number of denominations (described as "mainline" because they were strong along the mainline railroad out of Philadelphia) are experiencing sharp declines in membership. A few groups, Mormons, for example, continue to grow rapidly. The Catholic Church also continues to grow. We can recognize strong socioeconomic forces at work, for example, the growing tendency of middle-class families to have fewer children since the baby boom. As for the demographics of American society, total population is increasing at a rate matched by few denominational groups, population diversity is increasing, and proportions of minority populations are changing at different rates in different parts of the country. Increased immigration affects the statistics and accounts for some of the Catholic growth. Similarly, church membership on the whole is growing older on the average in most denominations.

A most helpful guide to this world of church demographics is an essay describing the factors that influence growth or decline. David Roozen and Jackson Carroll describe four arenas that may influence growth or decline:

Local factors internal to the congregation. How do the pastor and the congregation "get along"? How do the people of the congregation treat each other, and how welcoming are they to visitors or new people? How vital is their worship and how strong is the spirituality they practice?

Local factors external to the congregation. Does the community in which the congregation exists value religious traditions and churches? How much tension is there between groups of different classes or races in that community? How safe do people in the community feel? What are the patterns of weekend recreation? What image has that particular congregation projected over the years in that community?

National or regional factors internal to the denomination. What impact has the national image of the denomination had? What controversies or great projects is the denomination known for in the area? What is the character of the denomination-wide changes in theological position or worship? What theological stance has the denomination taken and how does it understand itself vis-à-vis the society? What is the public image of the denomination?

National or regional factors external to the denomination. What is the impact of economic and demographic conditions in the whole society? What are the societal factors of security or anxiety that influence the social order? How do people in society in general feel about the usefulness or trustworthiness of religious institutions? (Large parts of the

country, for example, that lie in the "Bible belt" find wide social affirmation of religion in the culture and find church a widely accepted, highly
valued ingredient in community life, whereas the Pacific Coast has many
areas with a more secular culture, giving less social support to religious
institutions in general or to those who are churchgoers).[15]

Finke and Stark see category 3—denominational factors—as being
the most influential to church membership demographics. My reading
of the data leads me to focus the spotlight on category 4, national or
regional factors external to the denomination. I believe something has
happened in American society overall that has changed the climate in
which the denominations operate.[16]

I see the membership curves, then, as being greatly influenced by
the culture we are in, which is why I foresee the leveling off and decline
of growth that has been experienced by the mainline churches as soon
spreading to other religious bodies. Only time itself can prove future pre-
dictions or projections. Indeed, one can hope my prediction is not true.
But that is how I read the signs of flattening membership and some early
indications of decline in some of the more rapidly growing denominations. In conversations with leaders in those denominations, I sense that
few of these churches are still feeling like "winners" in the growth wars.
An interesting theory that independently supports my feeling has been
provided by John and Sylvia Ronsvalle in what they call their Unified
Theory of Giving and Membership.[17] In this theory the authors link giving patterns and membership: In all denominations that experienced declining memberships, members' giving in proportion to their income
started to decrease five years before the membership figures dropped. In
denominations that have not yet experienced major losses in membership, they perceive a decline in percentage of income, beginning in 1985.

Because of data-collection obstacles discussed early in this chapter,
it will be a decade or two before we fully understand how these trends
play out.

What one can say unequivocally is that the mainline denominations
have suffered severe membership losses over the past twenty years, and
that there are no indications of a turnaround. If membership has anything
to do with financial health, these denominations are very close to "meltdown." Data from many other denominations indicate flattening growth
patterns, if not slight losses. To the extent that the financial health of
churches depends upon the tithes, pledges, and offerings of a solid core

membership, these signs of decreased membership are a foreboding threat to the future of the church.

Giving Levels

The actual data about giving to the churches have been as mysterious and unstudied as any part of the church's life. Only in the past decade have significant efforts been made to find out what is given by whom to what in the churches. A number of books in the nineties have filled in some of the gaps.[18]

The following two charts from John and Sylvia Ronsvalle (1994) provide a summary of the information pertinent to impending "meltdown."[19]

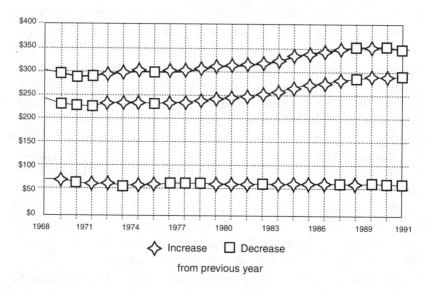

Patterns in Per Member Giving—Changes in Per Member Giving in Constant 1987 Dollars among Total Contributions, Congregational Finances and Benevolences, 1968-1991

◇ Increase   ☐ Decrease
from previous year

Source: empty tomb, inc., Champaign, IL, *The State of Church Giving Through 1994* by John and Sylvia Ronsvalle, © 1966, p. 11.

Let's look at the three lines across the chart.

The top line represents the amount (in constant 1987 dollars) given per member across the denominations reporting in the *Yearbook of American and Canadian Churches*. One fact stands out: Members of churches have been increasing their giving regularly from 1968-91. Of course this does not provide much more than a general conclusion, because the numbers being averaged out are so large and cover such a widespread population. But it is clear that average giving is going up.

The middle line is one we have been talking about as part of the problem: This line represents the part of the giving that goes to pay the costs of the congregation. Note that this increase is exactly parallel to the increase in giving. What this says is that all the increase in giving is required to maintain the costs in the congregation. What we cannot tell from these data is to what extent local congregations are more or less involved in "mission" activity today than they were two decades ago.

The bottom line indicates that all causes outside the local congregation have had a flat income line for twenty-five years. If your bishops and executives have had to pinch their budgets and cut staff, this line shows why. If your national denomination has had to "restructure" and "downsize," this is the reason. If seminaries and church agencies have become increasingly desperate for funds, this is the reason. Costs at those levels have increased, just as congregational costs have increased. But those parts of the institutional life have been having to "eat" the increases by cutting staff, dropping or curtailing programs, and doing whatever else a struggling bureaucracy can do to adjust to reduced resources. Many indicators of trouble described above reflect the financial pinch this line demonstrates graphically. I know of no data that suggest there will be much *change* in this pinch.

A second Ronsvalle chart offers another part of the picture and suggests a relationship between membership and giving:[20]

Per Member Giving as a Percentage of Income in 11 Denominations, 1921-1991

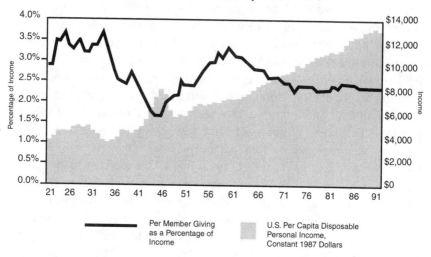

Per Member Giving as a Percentage of Income

U.S. Per Capita Disposable Personal Income, Constant 1987 Dollars

Source: empty tomb, inc., Champaign, IL, *The State of Church Giving Through 1994* by John and Sylvia Ronsvalle, © 1966, p. 11.

This graph has two major messages for our purposes.

First, the jagged black line describes the percentage of income that people gave to their churches in eleven denominations between 1921 and 1991. Again, one cannot tell anything about individual cases, because of the large samples and aggregations of data. But one can see that over that seventy-year period, giving has stayed fairly steady, between 2.5 and 3 percent of income. There have been fluctuations, but most yearly averages have been within that range. (I find it very interesting that percentage of giving stayed very high during the Depression.)

The other message of this graph, quantified on the right margin, shows that what the government defines as "disposable income" has been on a steady rise during those same years. People were giving 3 percent of their income to their churches back when they had—in the aggregate—only about four thousand dollars of disposable income. In 1991 they were giving 2.5 percent when they had nearly four times as much disposable income.

No one can tell precisely what all that means, but I find it provocative.

It says to me that in 1921 the congregations people belonged to rated high in their value systems; they gave a lot of money to the church out of very little income. Today, in contrast, each person has vastly more discretionary income. That increased amount of discretionary income is being used for many things, but not proportionately for the church.

This reinforces the Ronsvalles' argument that giving patterns may indicate that people are putting their interests in other places, and that congregations occupy less of their attention.

Most of the data noted here are suggestive, not conclusive. But what we see about membership and giving patterns makes this case:

> Continued budget support has held its own despite significant loss of membership, because many individual members have raised their dollar amount of giving.

> Almost all increases in church giving have gone to cover increased costs of local congregations.

> Overall giving of a proportion of income has not changed dramatically over the past seventy years, although the disposable income of church members has risen dramatically in the same period.

Aging Givers

The next dynamic is the critical piece in the picture. Again, in workshops I try to help people grasp this fact through their own knowledge and experience. I ask participants to jot down on paper the names (or initials) of the four or five strongest financial supporters in their congregations. I sometimes hear, "Oh, I don't know who they are," but I nevertheless push them to make a good guess. After a bit of silence, I ask, "Go down the list and put age by the names." I never ask to see the papers. But I remember the time I did this with a group of some 180 laypeople and clergy from about sixty congregations. There was an audible gasp! Most times I note a murmur of "wow." Their own localized calculations make the point: The strongest financial contributors to congregations are generally in the older generation, people whose children are raised and whose mortgages are paid. I do run into some congregations reporting strong giving in the twenty-to-thirty or thirty-to-forty age category, but those congregations are rare.

In most cases the people in these workshops realize how dependent they are upon the large pledges of their older members, in some cases very old members. And they also sense that in very few congregations are there large numbers of younger pledgers getting in line to take the place of the older ones when they move away or die. Congregations have become enormously dependent upon the tithes, gifts, and pledges of that portion of their membership over the age of sixty-five. I have heard so many anecdotal references to the impact on a small congregation of the loss of a single donor or single family that I have focused my worries around the depletion of donors over the age of seventy. A high percentage of the pledges those congregations currently depend on will be discontinued through death every year.

Many people hope that baby boomers, now entering their sixth decade, will fill the gap in giving as their children finish college and mortgages are paid up. Boomers can be very generous, some scholars say, but their patterns of giving do not reflect the institutional commitment and loyalty of the older generation. They seem more interested in giving to causes than to institutions. There is no guarantee that they will *not* become strong supporters of religious institutions, but there is little indication that they will.

New data, as reported in the book *Money Matters,* adds another worry.[21]

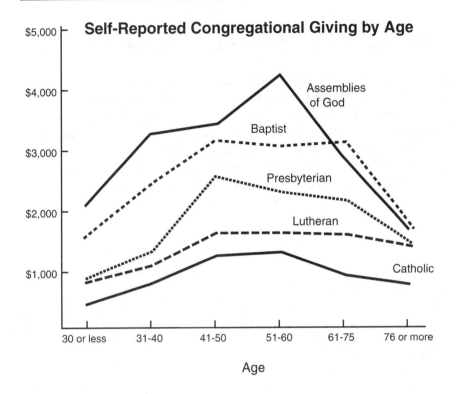

Self-Reported Congregational Giving by Age

Reproduced from *Money Matters* by Dean Hoge, Charles Zech, Patrick McNamara, and Michael J. Donahue. © 1966 by Westminster John Knox Press. Used by permission of Westminster John Knox Press.

Dean Hoge and his colleagues have identified trends that point to a peak of giving to local congregations when members are between the ages of fifty and sixty. If the data in *Money Matters* are better than my anecdotal worry, the crisis may be upon us much sooner than I had anticipated, as the baby boomers reach retirement.

My vision of the next few decades is very bleak. I see the lucky congregations managing to stay afloat for quite some time, doing just what they have been doing. But I see hundreds of congregations facing the loss of 20 to 50 percent of their pledged income in the next fifteen to twenty years. It will happen one congregation at a time; some this year will lose the two families that supported a third of their budget; others

will find the loss postponed a decade or so. And every time a congregation hits this wall, there will be an impact upon the regional office and
the denomination.

Put the forecasts and realities together—decreased numbers of members in the next decade, giving patterns that are stable but not growing,
and an aging base of current givers. I worry that I don't see many people
addressing the issues. They are like canoeists enjoying a lovely day on
the river, not realizing that the river is the Niagara and that the falls are a
couple of miles downstream. In terms of finances, churches are closing
in on Niagara and the current is getting stronger and faster.

CHAPTER 3

Uncertainties in Our Future

Who can tell what the future will bring? In the last chapter I tried to describe problems we can already see—problems that promise to make the financial situation of the churches less secure than it has been in the past.

In this chapter I want to point to areas in which there are threats that are less clear or certain. Some of these may never happen. Any of them may happen and may already have begun. Some may be more difficult than I can imagine.

I fear not only that I hear Niagara ahead of us; I also see clouds on the horizon that may well come to influence the future of the churches. I think of these clouds in three categories: funding glitches, entitlements, and unexploded bombs.[1]

Funding Glitches

Budget Creep

Budget creep is what I call a phenomenon I see often in organizational or family budget making. I use this phrase to describe the way items in budgets get redefined as times change, as pressures increase or decrease, and as once-clear values eventually grow muddy. On a practical and personal level, budget creep can be illustrated by a shopper in a supermarket noticing a videotape of a movie she's been dying to see. She throws it in the basket, thinking, *I'll just call it groceries.* Absolutely no bad intent, but if she doesn't look out, and if she keeps doing things like that, pretty soon a carefully planned grocery budget is way out of whack.

Here's a congregational example: One church had an unused piece of property, which the board agreed to lease out for a gas station—to the considerable anger of some church members. To cool tempers—and also because it fit their values—the board mandated that income from the property be used for two purposes: to pay for a parking lot upgrade and then entirely for local "outreach" projects. None of the income was intended to be used for salaries or ordinary expenses of the congregation. All went well at first. The parking lot project was completed, and for several years generous outreach grants went to important community projects.

Then several tough budget years came along, and budget creep started. The original policy-making board rotated into retirement and new people came on. The associate pastor's salary was redefined as outreach, because she led much of the congregational outreach into the community. Then the funds to buy and run a new (replacement) church bus were defined as outreach, because the bus could be used to help community groups. Gradually what had been earmarked for special purposes became indistinguishable from "budget," and a new line was added to the regular budget: "property income." There was—and usually is—no bad intent. Budget creep is just something that happens. Organizational memory gets lost in the pressure of current needs.

Budget creep happens slowly, yet over time it can make a substantial difference in the maintenance of an organization. The congregation I described above discovered that its regular annual commitments had crept up by about $80,000 (the money for the associate pastor's salary plus the running costs of the bus) without the board having clearly decided to do that. Please note that I hold no brief for never changing one's mind on budget matters. This congregation may have done exactly what it should have. The point is that without clear board action or considered thought about the consequences, the budget expanded so that future boards had the responsibility for $80,000 additional expenses for ordinary operations. The money was there, so they used it for good purposes. Money "migrated" from capital (property) to operational expenses. Nobody stole a dime, but the intended uses of resources shifted significantly. It would take a very sizable increase in pledged or tithed income to undo the migration. And nobody really thought it iimportant enough even to note in the minutes. The congregation "forgot" its earlier principle.

Budget shifts are slow and subtle—that's why I use the word *creeping* to describe them. One denomination's funding may illustrate the problem. Several years ago the General Commission on Ministry of the United Methodist Church, in carrying out its mandate to gather and share important information about the life of the denomination, did a provocative study of budgets over twenty years, from 1972 to 1993. To help mathematically challenged people like me, they converted their funds into constant dollars and divided the budgets out to show how a dollar given to the church was split among the different needs (which makes each point equivalent to 1 percent).

The following table represents what they discovered:[2]

The Local Church Dollar*

Keeping in mind that one cent of the local church dollar expended in 1994 represents about $34 million, the following comparisons of the allocation of that dollar amount are of interest:

	1973	1994
Of the amounts administered by		
local churches, totalling:	**78.7 cents**	**81.2 cents**
Capital Expenditures and Debt Liquidation	23.5	18.2
Program and Operating Expense	30.7	36.6
Pastoral Salaries and Expenses	23.1	23.9
Benevolences Paid Directly	1.3	2.5
Of the amounts administered by		
jurisdictions, areas, annual conferences		
and districts, totalling:	**14.4 cents**	**14.3 cents**
Clergy Support (including pension and benefit funds) and Connectional Administration Funds	7.9	9.8
Conference and Other Benevolences	6.5	4.6
Of the amounts administered by		
general agencies, totalling:	**5.3**	**3.8**
Clergy Support and Connectional Administration Funds	0.6	0.5
World Service and Other Apportioned Benevolences	3.3	2.2
The Advance and Other General Benevolences	1.4	1.1
Connectional Contributions Reported by		
Local United Methodist Women Units, Totalling:	**1.6**	**0.7**
Totals	**$1.00**	**$1.00**

*The information on this chart is provided from a public report of the General Council on Finance and Administration of the United Methodist Church in the United States of America. It lists the amounts of expenditures from each dollar received for the period from 1973 through 1994, adjusting the 1973 totals to eliminate the effects of inflation as measured by the Consumer Price Index.

In the four major categories, note the changes in twenty years. The percent of expenses for the local church has gone up a bit (which reflects cross-denominational findings of John and Sylvia Ronsvalle, 1994[3]), but the changes are not dramatic. There is a similar slight increase in the percentage of funds spent by the region (a small difference from the Ronsvalle findings), and a noticeable decrease of congregationally collected funds available for the national purposes of the church. The biggest change in a major category is the decrease in income from United Methodist Church Women. This may be particularly significant for the budget, because in most denominations the funds from women's organizations have traditionally been used for nonbudgeted front-line mission or outreach efforts.

Now consider the subhead categories, especially at the local-church level. Spending on "capital and indebtedness" dropped in twenty years by nearly 6 percent. That's an enormous change. What goes into that definition may differ from congregation to congregation, but it no doubt includes long-term investments, such as mortgage payments and replacing a roof or boiler. It might include buying property for expansion or relocation. In one way or another, it would support long-range purposes. Its intent would be to support the strong longevity of the church's fabric.

Expenditures noted on the next line, "program and operations," in the same time period increased by about the same amount! Another significant change. Program and operations generally refers to shorter-range commitments. Paying bills. Covering week-by-week program costs. Funding church activities and worship. My hunch is that most of what this line covers is important. I probably would have voted for it, and I would be proud to have my church doing whatever it was.

But look at the pattern: a significant shift from long-term investment to paying for current operations. Every organization occasionally or seasonally has to respond to short-term imperatives, but any organization that does so systematically over a long period is piling up trouble for the future. This illustrates how budget creep can be a cumulative pattern over time, changing the thrust of an organization.

Other subtle shifts occur in local congregational budgets. Here is an observation made regarding the same years as the Methodist report. The informant is a long-time staff person in the office of an Episcopal bishop in the Northeast:

. . . looking at finances in 1970, parish operating income still ex-
ceeded parish operating expenses. In 1990 the opposite was true.
Operating expenses [as defined in that diocese] are only local purposes and funds to the diocese. No outreach, maintenance, special
programs are included. In this diocese the apportionment (for mission
causes and diocesan/national expense) is a lower percentage now
than it was in 1970.

I would also note that in this diocese there were the equivalent of
sixteen fewer full time clergy positions in 1990 than in 1970. I think
(but cannot quantify) that parishes are a lot more energy conscious,
have cut secretary and sexton hours and have taken many other cost
cutting moves.[4]

To me, all this suggests conscientious struggle to patch up the trou-
blesome spots and adjust as best as is possible where costs are outrun-
ning income. But as that happens, the proportions within the budgets are
sliding. The proportions reflect the fact that congregational leaders are
responding to the most urgent needs and not necessarily to a set of clear
priorities.

Deferred Maintenance

Everybody knows about deferred maintenance; it is the way most of us
get through life. To illustrate: A few weeks ago the shower in our up-
stairs bathroom went on the blink. I couldn't shut it off. I didn't have
time to do anything about it just then. I was in and out of town, and we
had no scheduled guests, so I did a quick-fix—capped the line with a
temporary plug and went about my business. When things calmed down
and before the next guest arrived, I checked further. Discovering that the
problem was clearly beyond my skills, I phoned a plumber. Everybody
understands this mode of operation. Most home owners make select "I-
can-put-it-off-awhile" choices without thinking.

So do churches. Sometimes we calculatingly manage that way. We
present a budget that includes the expense of painting the education
building (say it's a big one—$20,000). Everybody knows it's a budget
trick. If the income doesn't come in on target, we'll just put it off and do
it next year. Or if the money does come in, we may still hold it off until
the end of the year—just in case. That's normal.

But there's trouble when replacement of aging boilers and roofs is put off for a year, then two, then a dozen. In bad cases real damage occurs, because the roof leaks or the heating plant collapses. City churches with many members "commuting" in from the suburbs suffer a lot this way, but so do small country churches. The thousands of churches built right after World War II are now over a half century old, and few of them can put their hands on the funds to bring their plants up to date. People in each community may have some sense of the size of the local problem, but I do not think anybody has a clue about how big the problem is overall. I do not know of a single denomination or even a judicatory that has even tried to estimate how much it would cost to repair its property, much less bring it up to current standards.

Habitual deferment of maintenance leads to disaster. It's like hope deferred, which makes the heart sick. Some churches live in hope that someday there will be money to fix it all up. My forecast of the future for most churches does not include the unexpected windfall that would make that strategy work. Looking at these data, a church executive told me, "Hope is a theological truth, but hope without planning is denial!"

Capital Drives for Operations

One fund-raising tool that has "worked" for churches for nearly fifty years is the capital funds drive. Such special appeals are rarely easy; they take lots and lots of energy and commitment; and they don't always hit their goals. But churches know how to do them and learned to do them for great projects—building a new church plant, establishing a seminary or college, building a conference center. Right after World War II many denominations launched great nationwide campaigns to rebuild churches that had not been repaired since before the Depression and to build new churches in sprawling suburbs.

As national and regional budgets hit the stresses of the seventies and eighties, the "capital drives" would better have been called "special campaigns"; the purposes for the funds shifted toward program expenses. (I see this as one form of budget creep.) The names of the drives were impressive: Major Mission Funding, Venture in Mission, the New Millennium Fund, the Fund for the Future. Impressive, sometimes heroic risks were taken to carry out those drives, and many people gave sacrificially.

There is reason to be proud of what was done. But much of the income was used for short-term projects and was not invested in such a way that the capital remains as a strength to those churches. Where, today, are the funds from those great campaigns? Or where are the strengthened operations or new tools for ministry that we thought the funds would give us? My hunch is that church administrators and leaders used capital funds because they did not have the discipline to cut programs and staff that we could no longer afford to continue.

Unexpected Costs of Operations

In 1972 the chaos in the Middle East sent the price of petroleum sky high. Ordinary congregations saw heating bills quadruple, then double. Churches used to paying a few hundred dollars a year for cheap oil heat suddenly, in the middle of a budget year, discovered monthly bills equaling the annual allocation for heat. Operational costs of physical structures blew our budgets out of the water. Until that time, church-people had overlooked what we now see as obvious: energy-saving equipment such as insulated windows and efficient boilers.

We continue to miss the lesson that time should have taught us; we don't plan defensively. When we carry out capital campaigns that are to provide new buildings or agencies, we rarely think of ramifications for the operations budgets. I know of any number of regional judicatories that in the past decade have raised substantial funds for a retreat center or young people's camp only to discover that they had overlooked the need to fund the operations that will occur there. I know of one such (fine) camp and conference center that has already begun to defer maintenance, because the staff and program costs of operating the facility had not been adequately planned for.

This kind of overlooking the obvious is doubly painful when the capital campaign falls short, as many do. I know of another conference center laboring under the debt of $100,000 that had to be borrowed to complete the building. Even though this center had made sound and careful plans for covering operating costs, it struggles to cover the unexpected additional costs of a mortgage.

Bequests as Windfalls

As I have worked with congregations—some with endowments and
many without—I have been surprised at the way many church boards
routinely use income from unencumbered bequests as a way to balance
the budget, to take care of some deferred maintenance, or to carry out a
project that didn't fit into the budget.

Note, I refer here to unencumbered bequests, which the donor leaves
to the church without specifying particular use. Legally, the church can
do whatever it wishes with those funds. But the prospects of this practice
leave me uncomfortable. One can imagine a church board facing tough
budget times looking over the congregation and being *tempted* to think
the words of the Fats Waller song, "I'll be glad when you're dead, you
rascal, you!"

I feel that bequests need special thought and concern, because they
are not an annual gift; they represent a lifetime. It may be legal to balance the budget with bequest income, but I am not sure that such a policy reflects well on how churches should treat member bequests.

I also am concerned with how such a policy can lead congregations
beyond the legal-but-questionable to the questionably legal. Budget
creep such as I mentioned earlier can push into the bequest arena. A
bequest for a congregation's educational program can get shunted over
to make up the difference when a capital drive for an education building
falls short of its goals. Everyone—including the donor—intended the
bequest's income to be used to pay for educational programming, but
when the million-dollar building campaign falls $100,000 short, some-
one wonders if the bequest could fill the gap. It is very difficult to keep
boundaries clear when pressing needs and strong values push toward
actions that seem so reasonable.

An Eroded Sense of Fiduciary Trusteeship

People who have to handle lots of other people's money generally know
what a slippery surface they are on. It is just so easy to make compro-
mises, to allow questionable practices to creep in, and to justify the mis-
handling of funds after the fact. Professionals in this field have, over the
years, developed elaborate systems of controls and supervision to make

sure that their decisions are made in accord with clear policy principles and are all out in the open. Fiduciary responsibility is one of the names we give this clarity. Trusteeship of funds is an acknowledged principle for all those who manage money.

Many of us do not have a lot of experience in managing large sums of other people's money and may not be as sensitive to the issues as are those who do it for a living. In past generations congregations have drawn upon the financial expertise of people in the business community—people for whom financial trusteeship in the church was one way of articulating their Christian faith. People like me, in our passion to "do programming," sometimes think those people have substituted trusteeship for their faith, so tightly have some held the purse strings! Relations between program people and financial managers in congregations often get testy. In actual fact, the churches are strongest when concern for program is balanced by trusteeship of the financial underpinnings of the institutional framework.

Since the fifties an admirable concern for broadening the base of congregational leadership has led to rotation of people serving on boards and committees. Limited tenure has brought thousands of members into active leadership roles. An unintended byproduct of "church democracy" has been a church leadership that is often not well trained or savvy when it comes to financial oversight and management. In my extensive work with congregations responsible for managing endowments—large and small—I often find the inexperienced trustees to be unclear about issues like the necessity for audits, potential conflicts of interest, or even ensuring that expenditures are consistent with the wishes of the donor.

Here I quote from a letter written by a manager and staff member of an Episcopal diocese for two decades, reflecting on the erosion of fiduciary trusteeship:

> The whole concept of trust funds and endowments has changed. Endowments were once trust funds. Today I wonder how many people even know what the concept "held in trust" means. . . . [P]arishes with endowments seem to have adopted a philosophy that they can spend principal and end up with the same endowment. Parishes with deficits are simply spending principal and counting on the stock market to rise by enough to leave them with the same endowment at the end of the year. Since around 1982 this plan (which was not

planned) has generally worked. In the 1990s most of our parishes with endowments have gotten quite satisfied with this financial strategy.[5]

Although the letter is about endowments, my focus is on the breakdown it describes in how trusteeship is understood by congregational leaders. Our pastors have not paid much attention to this deficit in leadership for two reasons: (1) In the tension between responsible trusteeship and responsible program leadership, their interests have been on the side of program; (2) Few pastors have passions about how financial management is carried out.[6] Pastors rarely act as if financial management issues are really as serious as issues they perceive as being pastoral and missional. They do not necessarily feel called to give strong leadership around financial management.

Ecclesiastical Doublespeak

This is the name I give to the way we talk about money and economics around churches. We act as if it is more important to keep up appearances than to communicate forthrightly and clearly. We say one thing to cover up something else. In his novel *1984,* George Orwell introduced us to "doublespeak," the public rhetoric in a society in which one thing was said and something else was meant. Once you are attuned to doublespeak, you can recognize the code language.

A most common example of this is found in public statements about budget deficits. A headline from the *Presbyterian Outlook* (3 March 1997) is a case in point: "GAC General Assembly Council, the national executive committee Approves 1998-9 Mission Budgets, Expecting Increased Giving."

A budget press release about the 1997 budget adds another element: "GAC Increases Mission Budgets in Wake of 1996 Surplus." Although the headline sounds optimistic, details in the press release and the article reveal another story. It seems that drastic midyear shortages of income made it necessary to slice the 1996 budget to the bone. Then toward year-end more money came in than the crisis managers had expected. So there was a little "extra" that could be allocated to bolster the 1997 income. There is more. Because they had cut income projections by 7 percent for 1996, they had cut that amount for 1997. Looking at what had happened in 1996, they decided they could revise the 1997 budget and cut income by only 5 percent. So a 2 percent "increase" is announced in addition to a windfall from 1996.

What does it mean? That there is less money budgeted for program now than had been planned and budgeted two years previously. Take out the doublespeak about increased mission giving. (Translation: The cut is not as bad as we thought it would be.) Take out the doublespeak about "surplus" for 1996. (Translation: When we cut all those jobs and money, we should have cut, but we cut too much. Now we can spend it.) Not quite as bad as everyone had thought. The mission budget for 1997 actually was a significant decrease from what had been hoped even at the beginning of the year.

The news is about readjusting losses, but the rhetoric is about "gains" and "increases." That is ecclesiastical doublespeak.

My example may seem unfairly to target Presbyterians, because theirs is the most recent case I have seen. But I find this kind of doublespeak endemic in the denominations. Losses are described as gains in denomination after denomination. Cuts in program are described as improvements in strategy. Downsizing is heralded as a new vision of mission.

Here is another example, from the Evangelical Lutheran Church in America. The denominational president told his constituency: "I am pleased that we have achieved stability in our churchwide ministries. *We are operating with a balanced churchwide budget, despite far less income than was anticipated....*[7]

The lead statement of the presidential annual report is how well the denomination is doing. That is the section that makes the headlines and sets the stage. Denominational leadership seems to require this spin to be put on bad economic news. Then, in the follow-up pages, this particular president conveys a grimmer message:

> But as we look at the giving patterns of our members we cannot help but feel great distress. In spite of the calls for greater giving over many, many years, our average member gives only 2 to 3 percent of spendable income for all charitable causes, including the church. And the trend is toward giving less to the mission beyond the local church—a trend that began more than 30 years ago.

He continues, with a realistic statement about what the cuts had cost the denomination:

> Reduced income, however, has meant that we are not doing as much as we had envisioned at the beginning of our church's life. We have fewer missionaries; we are starting fewer new congregations; we are giving less to our seminaries, colleges, and campus ministries; scholarships for needy students have been reduced; our support for ecumenical commitments for Lutheran World Federation is far less than it should be. I could add more.

One gets the message by "digging," but the lead message is that we have done very well.

This sugar-coating of the financial situation in the churches is second nature. Public relations, not the need for clear, unambiguous messages, directs our communication. It is not hard to figure why members in the pews are surprised to find out that there are very serious problems across the board in the financing of religious institutions.

We don't talk straight about money.

Entitlements

We are not used to talking about *entitlements* in a church context, though the word is widely used in the secular arena, to describe things we come to take for granted, things we expect to be ours by right. Americans clearly see Social Security as an entitlement, something nobody will be allowed to take away from them. Similarly, Americans expect some kind of medical care.

Conflicts over perceived entitlements run deep. Labor and employers are often at odds about what is and is not an entitlement—even down to the issue of basic job security. In recent years the "entitlement" of advancement and promotion has sometimes conflicted with an equally passionately held entitlement to nondiscriminatory personnel policies. One of the most difficult areas of labor relations has been about medical benefits for retirees. What unions saw as an entitlement, the company found it could not guarantee. The feuds have been bitter: once a benefit is perceived to be an entitlement, any attempt to cut back–for whatever reason–feels like betrayal.

I use the word *entitlement* with churches to spotlight some of the areas in which passionate disagreements seem unavoidable. People believe long-term commitments have been made, but eventually there are not enough resources to support an open-ended guarantee.

Entitlements feel like promises. And church people do not like to break promises—or have them broken. Yet today the financial condition and the shape of our institutional life calls into question our ability to keep some of the promises we have made. For people like us, who believe in keeping our word, that is serious.

I here note several areas in which apparent entitlements may have to be reconsidered in the future: program and institutional entitlements and jobs, salaries, and benefits entitlements. In some cases reconsideration has already begun.

Program and Institutional Entitlements

Churches can develop such deep commitments to a specific program that the program takes on the character of an entitlement, and any effort to change it sparks resentment, feelings of betrayal, and deep opposition. The specific program involved differs with the denomination and the circumstances.

Churches have long had commitments to caring for those in need. But during the eighties political changes required even more effort from nonprofits to feed the hungry and house the homeless. Thousands of churches stepped forward to respond to this calling. Responding, however, had its costs. Many congregations discovered that these new programs put stress on their buildings, often not designed for heavy seven-day-a-week use. It stressed congregational staffs. It stressed church volunteers at a time when the volunteer pool was shrinking because women were returning to the workforce. But church after church, synagogue after synagogue, stepped up to bat and began new ministries or expanded old ones.

The ministries have been maintained now for nearly twenty years. Despite the fact that buildings and people are worn and torn, having depleted their beginning capital of energy and vitality, the programs have come to be "givens," entitlements not only to the service recipients, but also to the spiritual life of the at-risk congregations. There are two "entitlements" here. The first is the entitlement of the recipient of the ministry. Although that is important in itself, what I want to call attention to is the *other* entitlement—that of church members' entitlement to *give* service and ministry. That joyful entitlement is threatened by our poor management of people and buildings, overstressing both.

Over the past three decades most of the denominations have also discovered that their deep commitments to foreign missions have come into conflict with an inability to fund those commitments. To cut back, as has been inevitable in many cases, is to offend those loyal members who see this not just as a matter of dollars and cents but as a requirement. An entitlement for their soul's sake, no less.

Those who feel a program to be so important as to be an entitlement are among our most valuable and committed members, and they are not patient when the entitlement they affirm is violated. There is little room for negotiation when entitlement is seen to be at stake.

Many church members have come to feel that their current church "arrangement" will last "forever." If they have had pastors in the past, they will have them in the future. If they have had access to a judicatory staff (with or without a bishop, according to denominational polity), that access will continue. If there have been institutions of learning for the young, they will be there for children and grandchildren. If there have been opportunities for worship in a local church building, those opportunities will remain.

This sense of entitlement to one's accustomed institutional system sometimes leads to abuse of endowments. When a bequest is made to a congregation that is in declining health, members may feel they are entitled to use the bequest to maintain all the accouterments of a "full-service" congregation. Such congregations use the bequest or endowment simply to survive, subsidizing a narrow, in-grown life and vision. Such actions give a bad name to congregational endowments and discourage others from making such gifts. The problem is the sense of entitlement that makes the people selfishly want to preserve a dying institution for their own enjoyment.

I believe that many people across the country will see those seemingly safe entitlements being called into question within the next generation. Many small communities will be unable to maintain anything like the "church" they know and love today.

Jobs, Salaries, and Benefits as Entitlements

The greatest entitlement issue facing the church is that of clergy feeling they are "due" a job and the benefits that go with it. In years past this was a spoken entitlement. Bishops and executives told prospective clergy that they could expect a life-long opportunity to serve the churches in a salaried position. More recently, increasingly aware that job security is no longer a possibility for many denominations, such promises are rarely made out loud. More often than church leaders intend, however, the unspoken promise is assumed to be operative by the candidate for ordination.

Within the United Methodist Church, for example, there is still a formal commitment to treat ordination as entitlement to a job—a commitment that worries many of the budget makers I know in that denomination. Declining membership could well affect that entitlement in the next decade.

The reality—that no such entitlement truly exists in any other denomination—comes as a distinct, unwelcome shock to many pastors, and unfortunately at the very worst time: when their current pastorate ends and they need a new job.

The person committing himself or herself to three years of graduate training often assumes that the job is there for them. Many are heartbroken and some angry when they find the truth that some denominations have twice as many ordained people as they have positions. The sense of betrayal is intense. Even though there may have been no overt misleading, the human cost can be high. The problem exists in another way for "hard-to-place" pastors (a distressing phrase used in denominational structures for nonwhite, female, or over-fifty white male pastors).

If I am even close in my estimates of what lies ahead for the financial structures of the churches, I expect that as many as 25 percent of the pastors now enjoying paid full-time positions in congregations will discover in the next twenty years that what they thought to be a life-time entitlement has come to an end.

The costs I see here are costs of personal dislocation and disappointment, but also the cost of alienation of some of our finest people who discover they are unemployed or underemployed by the institution they sacrificed to serve.

For many, the front edge of the clergy entitlement problem lies in the issue of medical insurance costs. In the fifties and sixties, when medical insurance was inexpensive and church budgets were flush, churches made decisions to provide medical insurance to clergy and to pay all or part of the costs. Congregational or denominational coverage of medical insurance became a standard part of the "package" clergy expected. But in the eighties and nineties, those costs have escalated rapidly. Several regional judicatories I have worked with have been startled by increases of as much as 50 percent in a single year. More and more of the costs of insurance and medical expenses are now being passed on to individual pastors, some of whom are resentful at what seems to be reneging on a promise. In the United Methodist Church, these costs have been shifted from regional budgets to local budgets. Doubly sensitive is the issue of medical insurance costs for retired pastors.[8] Looking ahead, it is clear that medical costs will continue to rise, perhaps at a less rapid rate. But rise they will, and every rise will cause tension and result in difficult decisions.

Entitlements Summary

Entitlements come in many types and sizes. When budgets are being pared and "nonessentials" are being dropped, it is not always easy to determine when an entitlement has been stepped on. Indeed, what is one person's nonessential may be a highly charged entitlement for others.

The interaction between entitlements is also complex. In 1995 Presbyterian friends told me there was a saying going around: that the previous year's cuts in mission budget exactly equaled the increases in costs of medical insurance.

In 1996 I worked with a judicatory that had, with deep commitment, initiated four congregations among ethnic populations in the late eighties, only to discover that financial shortfalls in three of the congregations were threatening the operations of the judicatory. The diminishing budget put the judicatory family in a position of having to make terribly painful decisions about conflicting senses of entitlement.

In one sense we are simply talking about the priority choices all institutions have to make when needs outstrip resources. My use of the term *entitlement* here underlines the fact that some choices we have to make involve very deep senses of commitment to a program or a person or an institutional understanding.

Every time someone's assumed entitlement is violated, there is a basic sense of betrayal of values. In coming years, as we experience continuing budget difficulties, we will have to face changes in our entitlement definitions. Every time that happens, members of the church experience earthquakes. How many and how severe those earthquakes will be is unpredictable. What is predictable is that they will occur, perhaps more frequently than in the past.

Unexploded Bombs

A couple of years ago the people in the lovely Spring Valley section of Washington, D.C.—large urban homes on rolling lots full of dogwoods and azaleas—woke up to distressing news. Kids playing in backyards had discovered a couple of old rusted grenades. The grenades were found to be live, though fortunately they did not go off. It seems sometime before World War II, war games, complete with live ammunition, had been played out in Spring Valley. Now, for several weeks, these fashionable homes had to be evacuated while specialists dug all around for ammunition. The neighborhood looked pretty peaceful, but until the hidden explosives were found and disarmed, lives were in jeopardy.

At the end of modern wars, the countryside is sometimes littered with artillery shells and bombs that did not explode. Some of them are dead—duds from the beginning. Others are quite alive and are likely to explode unexpectedly if jostled by someone nearby. And what about those that are assumed to be dead but could explode at any time?

As I have tried to understand the dilemmas we face in church finances, I have often thought of Spring Valley. I have come to feel that we have in our "neighborhood" a number of shells or bombs that have not gone off, but that may at any moment. As in Spring Valley, it may be that all of them can eventually be removed without harm. Or, as still happens in Afghanistan and Vietnam, these shells might still explode, changing lives forever.

Bomb 1: Governmental Tax Policies

Let me name and describe a number of different ways that future actions on tax policy could affect our churches.

Property Taxes

In most communities there is a general acceptance that buildings of religious groups should be free of some tax burdens, because of the important functions the churches carry out in the community in addition to specifically religious functions. But as communities get hard-pressed to provide the police, sewer, and transportation services that citizens demand, local political leaders will be tempted to look longingly at property not taxed because of the religious exemption.

In addition, many people who have no religious affiliation or even appreciation are beginning to demand that religious groups help pay for community services. Where such pressure is strong, some communities are likely to face policy changes in the near future. That is already happening in some places in one way or another. The following are actual examples:

Churches are asked to make a payment for community services (water, sewer, police, or some combination) "in lieu of taxes." In some cases the payments are substantial and are almost in the form of assessments.

Certain kinds of church property (formerly tax-exempt) are put on the tax rolls while others remain off. Pastors' homes, educational buildings, and "meeting halls" tend to go on the rolls before "worship" space. Most property the church owns but rents out is already on tax rolls.

Office buildings the church uses (judicatory offices, educational institution offices) are often placed directly on tax rolls just as any other office building would be.

Conference centers, struggling to remain solvent, rent their facilities for business retreats and discover they may have tipped a local understanding about the difference between "profit" and "not-for-profit." They can end up with substantial new taxes.

Questions are quickly raised when a church purchases property for expansion—a building for outreach purposes, space for education, or even an empty lot for parking. Is it to be exempt from taxes or not? A church I work with recently purchased a next-door store building to provide much-needed education space. The city is trying to figure out if the tax-paying department store can be changed to a nontaxed property. The answers make a real difference!

Decisions that change the tax-exempt nature of church property are now being made by governmental bodies across the country. Local option seems to be the rule, and the weight is still on the side of generous exemptions. But many churches that have never had to consider tax payments on property are likely to have to face that question in coming years.

A strong statewide campaign in Colorado was mounted in 1996 to put all nonprofit and religious property on tax rolls. Although that initiative failed, it should have been a wake-up call to all of us: There is an increasing voice—and not just among the fringe people who fight any forms of religion—saying that it is not fair for businesses and individuals to pay for police and fire service, road maintenance, and water, sewer, and trash removal services for the nonprofit world. Many churches voluntarily provide payment to city or county to cover police, fire, and sewer services.

A strong swing toward placing more church property on tax rolls would have an immediate and serious impact upon hundreds of financially marginal congregations, especially city congregations with large building plants. The pressure for change is strongest in cities, as political leaders desperately seek to keep their cities solvent. This bomb is not exactly unexploded. It is popping even now.

Clergy Housing Allowance Deduction

Federal tax policies have long had a provision that permits a clergyperson to be paid a housing allowance by the congregation or agency as part of the employment package. The housing allowance can be substantial if the congregation does not provide a parsonage. Even if there *is* a parsonage, there may be a payment for some or all utilities in the church-provided house as part of an employment package. That housing allowance, considered nontaxable income, can be a substantial financial benefit to clergy. The justification for the exemption has been deemed plausible, because the clergyperson is "required" by the work to live close to the congregation. It is further justified in that many clergy come to the end of a career without a permanent home because of the peripatetic character of their profession.

There are arguments for and against this policy.[9] No matter how one feels about it, it is, nevertheless, a matter of public policy that affects clergy and congregations economically. What happens if that policy changes?

In the past few decades every time Congress has considered tax revision, this provision has come up for review. Several times it has come close to being revoked. I would not be surprised if Congress were to decide to remove this exemption and to declare all clergy housing allowances to be fully taxable.

I name this as an unexploded bomb, because of the consequences to clergy and churches if this policy changes. The impact would be an immediate cut in effective income for most clergy, the new tax on "housing allowance" coming out of their total income. A new tax expense of several thousand dollars a year would be a significant burden for many clergy families.

Many congregations would want to help their clergy by a compensating increase in stipend, but poorer congregations could not do so. Some congregations might well divert the extra out of outreach or mission budgets. If the bomb goes off, there would be consequences.

Charitable Deductions

No government policy on taxation is as critical to the income of religious institutions as the provision that allows contributions to religious and charitable institutions as itemized deductions from income for tax purposes. Because this policy has been central to our values as a country longer than it has been part of any tax code, it is unlikely that it will ever be totally eliminated. Thousands of educational and nonprofit organizations count on this deduction as a motivating factor in generating contributions that help them do the community-building work so central to our society.

Germany has a much more proactive policy, with the government collecting taxes *for* religious organizations—a leftover medieval practice that also, since World War II, serves to respond to sensitivity about the government's interference with religion. Their policy is radically different from ours, but both rest on an affirmation of the value of religious organizations to the life of the country. With an erosion of public support for religion, there is a public push for the German government to change its proactive policy. If the current system is overruled, it will be interesting to see if an American-style tax deduction for voluntary contributions will become the new law. I note two further points about the German tax system.

First, the impact of public concern about tax policy is real. If the public ceases to support a particular way in which a government relates to charitable and religious organizations, the political process will eventually change that way of relating. We are not in the same position as the Germans. Support for our arrangement is widespread, although there are signs it is not as fully supported as it was several decades ago. And of course in a pluralistic, secular society, the German policy is harder to defend than is our policy of tax deduction for voluntary contribution.

Second, this potential change of policy in Germany has its own impact upon us. Major ecumenical agencies and world mission efforts have been funded largely by German churches, using the funds collected by their governments. Some 40 percent of World Council of Churches income comes from Germany. Suppose that were reduced significantly. Would American churches step into the breach? Could they? Should they? And what would our responsibility be if the churches of Germany were placed at risk by a sharp reduction in income? What will happen to American churches if German church funding for international mission causes is reduced?

I know of no government with a policy of taxation more friendly to charitable causes and religious institutions than the United States. Yet within recent years a number of adjustments to this provision of the tax codes have been proposed. Some limits have been placed and are likely to continue to be placed limiting certain kinds of gifts—of art or capital. There has been serious discussion of flat-tax proposals that would have great impact on all kinds of contributions. One limit already in place is the IRS practice of targeting for audit those who sharply increase their gifts or whose gifts surpass an IRS guideline.

Even minor adjustments that seem very sensible can be difficult to manage in unsophisticated church offices. A case in point was the ruling that a taxpayer needs a letter substantiating any gift of $250 or more. No one can argue with the ruling, but I know plenty of congregations where such letters do not go out unless the pastor sits down and types them—an interesting redirection of pastoral skills, precipitated by a minor adjustment to the tax policy!

I see this as the bomb that is probably least likely to explode massively or disastrously; there is still too much general public agreement on the policy and too many strong organizations that would fight radical change. And yet I scratch my head in wonder that I see virtually no advanced thinking in churches about alternative future funding options. Even if the bomb does not go off, firecrackers in this area have impact on all of us.

Bomb 2: Misappropriation of Funds

Across the churches in recent years, many people and groups have felt betrayed by the misuse of financial resources. The unexploded bomb is the impact of real or perceived misuse on people's willingness to provide gifts, offerings, pledges, and tithes to support church work. The issue is misuse of funds. The bomb is what that does to the element of trust, without which organizations cannot long continue. Let me comment on two kinds of misuse of funds.

Differences in Priorities

People give resources to their churches out of a variety of motives. Often —unless there is a fund drive for a specific purpose—the gifts are both generous and uncomplicated. When I put a check in the envelope and place it in the alms basin in my church, I have only a general idea how the money will be used. I have probably seen a budget and feel comfortable with it, but I don't remember a lot about it. We have an elected parish board (a vestry) that manages all that. I guess I don't want to know much more than I do. Our pastor and staff get paid; the heat works in the winter and the air conditioning in the summer. The music sounds great, and the worship is there when I need it. I think a fair percentage is set aside for feeding programs and for the homeless shelter at the parish.

We fulfill our obligations to share in the larger mission causes of our denomination. That makes me a happy camper. There are millions like me.

Suppose, though, that I found out that the vestry decided to have its vestry retreat at a posh resort on Bermuda, using parish funds to pay for it. You can imagine how I would feel. First, probably, simple envy (after all, *I've* never been to Bermuda.) Next, and not long after, sheer screaming anger. "What do they mean taking our parish money for such a boondoggle?" I don't know what all I'd actually *do,* but I probably wouldn't listen to their reasons. I probably would take a long hard look at what I'd pledge the next year. I might phone the parish office to get a copy of the budget and go through it with a fine-tooth comb.

This is an absurd scenario[10]—if you know our vestry. I use the example to put you in touch with the personal dynamic of it. I have a picture in my head of what the church is all about, and Bermuda junkets are not a part of it. As long as what the church board and staff do is consistent with the picture I have in my head, they can do pretty much what they want to, and I'd applaud. If, however, something like this Bermuda scenario happened that affected my ability to trust the leadership, it would change my feelings about the check I put in an envelope.

When a gap grows too wide between what I understand the church to be about and how the church uses my gifts, I have a problem and so does the church. In most cases I'm able to be reasonable. If I have high regard for the mission work of the churches in Africa and our parish support is switched to the mission schools in Central America, I probably could get on board, but I need help. If I am not helped to understand the need for the change, I may feel that some elite is being cavalier about my contributions.

When the system works, I trust my vestry. And the bishop. And all those other agencies and groups. And I'd rather they not bother me with questionnaires polling what I want the church to do. I want them to go on and see to the work of the church.

But when time after time I get surprised, it's different. When I find that my contributions are being used consistently for things I had no idea they were being used for—then I have a problem and so has the church. I stop trusting them and want to micro manage all their budget decisions.

All this is a polite way to say that just such a gap has developed—a large and painful gap—in trust between the givers of the funds and those who expend the funds of many denominations.[11] I genuinely believe that

those who make the spending decisions have almost always based their decisions on deep spiritual understandings and with mission strategies clearly in mind. But they have allowed terrible gaps to develop between what they were doing and what the donors thought they were doing. The gaps have eroded trust. As I noted in *Transforming Congregations for the Future:*

> The public media occasionally step into this gap to the dismay of religious leaders. Every decade or so *Reader's Digest* publishes an article about what the World Council of Churches or the National Council of Churches or one or another of the denominations is *really* doing with the donations it receives. "The people in the pew" give a loud cry because they have not known that their church leaders have changed programs. The church leaders get equally upset, thinking that important mission concerns are being undercut. Both have a point. But . . . my point lies in the fact that our religious leaders have not felt accountable for their choices. In their enthusiasm for important mission initiatives, they have acted like intellectual elites. At their worst, some of them have actually felt contempt for the narrow vision of some of the donors, and they have felt justified in using the funds in ways those donors would never support.

Most people can remember classic cases when they felt betrayed by the surprise news: when the Presbyterian church "gave all that money to Angela Davis"; when they learned from the morning headlines that their denomination was investing in a major social change initiative in their own town. Still today I find many church groups where feelings are quite raw about "that Minneapolis theology conference" in 1996.

Sometimes the surprise becomes a firestorm, with ultimatums, letters and speeches of protest, even disruption of church assemblies. There are denominations in which large groups have had so many such surprises that protest organizations have grown up to be watchdogs on the use of funds. When trust reaches that level, church meetings begin to look like guerrilla warfare.

This gap between what leaders see and what members see as be mission priorities is significant in every denomination with which I am familiar. There is no way to guess what this gap "costs" in reduced giving, but my guess is that it is considerable. The greater cost may be the

long-term one of trying to rebuild trust. That takes time and energy and a willingness to communicate with those with whom you differ. National and regional staffs have severely limited time and energy, but the real problem is that in too many cases the loss of trust has gone so far that people who oppose each other on mission strategy have stopped being able to talk to each other. Presbyterians, United Methodists, Episcopalians, Catholics, and Southern Baptists have all felt this polarization in the past few years.

Designated Funds

The second category I list under "misuse of funds" is another matter entirely. Many congregations, judicatories, national church agencies, schools, seminaries, and colleges have been given funds in trust for special purposes—from repairing buildings to paying pastors' salaries to providing scholarships or grants for mission purposes.

By accepting the funds, the church accepts the donor's stipulations about how the funds should be spent. It is not difficult for the original sharp purpose of the gift to become diffuse a generation or two later. Let's say there was a trust fund to replace the pastor's horse-drawn buggy every few years. I would expect this trust eventually would be included in the pastor's travel allowance. That allocation may be obvious. But what of funds given to pursue a mission concern when that mission is no longer in existence? Administrators and managers generally try to use the funds for the thing they can identify as nearest to the donor's purpose, but it is not always an easy call. Should a trust fund specified for work at a mission center for one tribe of Native Americans be used for a similar center for another tribe when the first center is no longer needed? Who should make such decisions and when?

"Budget creep" happens here with a vengeance. When projects with a strong and loyal constituency run out of money, there is a strong temptation to transfer income from the trust funds—just rewrite the purposes of the project to describe it in the terms of the trust. Over time some trust funds come to be treated as "discretionary program funds" at the call of program managers.

It is best to keep some boundaries and constructive tension between those holding the funds in trust and those who spend the funds, but that

is no guarantee of easy decision making. The Presbyterian Foundation (which has responsibility to see that many of the trust funds of that denomination are managed, invested, and spent in accord with the wishes of the donor) works in close collaboration with the General Assembly staff (which has responsibility for spending the allocated income). Even with all good intent, those two groups had some tensions in 1996, renegotiating relationships so that the intent of the donors would be demonstrably honored. Every now and then court cases test how churches use their trusts; in 1997 such a case was brought within the Episcopal Church about its use of trusts. In the Episcopal case, the boundaries between managing the funds and spending the income are not as clearly defined and separated as they are in the Presbyterian Church.

Wherever there is a question about use of trust funds—whether there is a court case or not—confidence in the financial system is shaken. This second form of potential misuse of funds is not as big an unexploded bomb as some I have described, but it could be if word got around that abuse of trust funds was widespread.

My digging around has given me no evidence of such widespread abuse, but three factors give me pause: (1) Clergy as a group, along with many other church leaders, tend to think of audits as necessary evils, preferring to trust everyone to do the right thing, a stance that says much for their belief in and trust of the people they work with, but causes them to overlook an important resource for management. Audits are not just a way to catch crooks! (2) In times of financial cutbacks, there is a tremendous undertow sucking resources from wherever they can be found to fund "critical" programs. I am not sure there is enough awareness of the dangers of "borrowing" from one fund to carry out critical programs. (3) The structural boundaries between the responsibility of carrying out the will of the donor and the program responsibility to spend the resources are sometimes fuzzy, leaving open the possibility of misunderstandings and misinterpretations.

These systemic weaknesses in the arrangements to keep faith with the purposes of donor's wishes are not likely to explode, but they have real potential to be a divisive issue in the future. I do wonder why little is done about it. We seem to have another hint of a characteristic myopia around financial matters. Once again, we see evidence of churches filled with responsible people, somehow not paying attention to this area.

Bomb 3: Embezzlement

When I first started asking about financial problems in the churches, nobody told me about embezzlement. I picked it up in newspapers— usually as "local news." In the characteristic news account, some local person is accused of (or arrested for) making off with funds from a local church, church agency, or judicatory. It is often clear that someone handling money was not supervised very well, and, under the pressure of a looming mortgage payment or tuition bill, "borrowed" a few thousand dollars with full intention of paying it back. Sometimes the story goes further, with the borrower caught in a continuing cycle, getting in deeper and deeper each month and unable to pay it back. Such stories reek with pain and tragedy. The one "caught" is often a trusted and loved member of the congregation. I have known boards of congregations to be tied in knots about what to do—whether to make the dear old lady sell her house to pay off the debt, whether to send her to jail, or whether to "forgive." No decision seems to be adequate. Once it happens, nothing seems able to set it right.

A complicating factor is that this behavior makes some people absolutely furious. The behavior is unquestionably wrong and should be condemned. But I've noted that this particular bad behavior triggers irrational anger in some people in such a way that the life of the congregation can be poisoned. Those who have been there know what I am talking about; the purely financial part of this kind of behavior is one thing, but it can explode relationships within the congregation.

Stories like this are usually kept pretty private. As I asked questions, it seemed that everybody knows of cases, but most do not become public. Few people will write down what they will tell me on the telephone. When I ask bishops or executives about it, their eyes roll back. Usually they can tell me anecdotes about several; their judicatory treasurers tell me about others. I hear lots of "don't quote me" language.

I believe hundreds of these cases occur every year; I would not be surprised if there were thousands. A judicatory that does not have at least one a year is a lucky one. And this says nothing of the many more that may remain unknown forever.

What do I mean by that? One Episcopal bishop told me of a church in his diocese that barely survived year after year. One summer the long-time treasurer was killed in a hunting accident. That year the church had a surplus of $50,000. The bishop said, "Loren, I don't want to know what was going on there." I hear similar stories of miraculous turnarounds when money-handlers take jobs in far-off cities. And about clergy going on sabbaticals or moving away, after which the financial situation radically improves. Again, nobody seems to want to "know what happened." Another Episcopal bishop told me that he suspected that 10 percent of the congregations in his diocese had experienced some kind of embezzlement over the past decade.

Just a few years ago we treated another widespread illness in the church with similar silence. That was about a ghastly pattern of power abuse—sexual abuse. The predominately male leadership of the churches sometimes seemed to wink at the abuse. People gossiped about it and even told jokes but did not seem to recognize it as a violation of something sacred.

This issue is about financial abuse. I cannot put the church's silence about misuse of funds in the same realm of personal abuse and tragedy, but it surely is an area in which we are covering up the truth, perhaps afraid of what we will find out. I believe it, too, is a case of irresponsibility in our leadership. Clergy and church leaders will tell jokes and anecdotes about embezzlements, but they do not seem to see them as serious, systemic problems.

We have not set standards and cared about them in the area of financial management. We have not cared about these boundaries enough to see that they are protected. Will this become an exploding bomb? I believe there is more explosive power in these minor local peccadilloes than we expect.

But let's look at the next step up—the big-time embezzlers. The small-time cases often get settled one way or another on the local scene. But who hasn't heard of spectacular cases in which somebody made off with barrels of the church's money? The big ones make it into the national media, but virtually no one looks at the total picture. Diane Winston of Princeton University wrote the most comprehensive public coverage I have seen on this issue, published in the *Dallas Morning News* (17 August 1996). I have never seen a follow-up article or any other national note of this phenomenon. In that article she lists "the big ones" she had uncovered. (The year indicates when the case was resolved.)[12]

1996	Ellen Cooke,	$2.2 million
	treasurer of the Episcopal Church	
1996	Martin Greenlaw,	$200,000
	Catholic priest, San Francisco	
1994	Mollie Brusstar,	$65,000
	Catholic diocesan administrator, Virginia	
1994	Michael Romanowski,	$275,000
	Catholic deacon, Denver	
1994	Donald Lusby,	$142,606
	parish bookkeeper, ELCA, Buffalo	
1993	John C. Weber,	$1 million
	Catholic diocesan accountant, Delaware	
1993	John Sansom,	$700,443
	church treasurer, Church of Christ	
	Pensacola, Florida	
1992	Anthony Franjone,	$1.5 million
	comptroller, Catholic diocese, Buffalo	
1992	Frederick Keppler,	$212,187
	comptroller, Catholic diocese, Vermont	

I suspect that the cases listed represent only the tip of the iceberg. Since I read the article, I have seen several dozen other stories reported in newspapers; each deals with a single local case.

For my purposes, however, it is not the number of dollars or the number of cases that is important. The issue ecame clear to me in conversations with Episcopalians across the country in the aftermath of the Ellen Cooke embezzlement trial.

What I found was not much concern about the money; everyone pretty well assumed that insurance and repayment would cover most of it. I found a quiet fury, a bitterness that was more widespread than I had imagined. Some of it was directed at Ellen Cooke, but most was indiscriminately spread over the presiding bishop, "all those bureaucrats," and almost anything one didn't like about one's own bishop or pastor or anyone else in positions of religious leadership.

The embezzlement may have been in dollars, but the cost to the church was in trust. That is the bombshell problem for the churches. It may be that no system can be constructed that will thwart a really skilled thief, but I do not see any signs of system-wide efforts to reduce this problem—except in the immediate aftermath of an embezzlement.

A second cost of embezzlement is the time and energy of church leaders. When an embezzlement breaks, the work begins with lawyers, auditors, and insurance companies. It goes without saying that such professional services can cost plenty in terms of dollars. It also drains a lot of energy from church leaders. Bishops, pastors, and lay leaders who have been through an embezzlement look shell-shocked when it is over.

As of now, this matter hides behind a curtain of silence, just as sexual abuse did two decades ago. I wonder why we refuse to take it seriously. If we could learn the true size of the issue, I suspect that we would find it a very big one.[13]

Bomb 4: Litigation Costs

Churches never used to have to worry about the costs of litigation. Someone in the congregation usually was a lawyer or knew a lawyer who would do minor tasks for no charge. Judicatories frequently had appointed legal counsel (sometimes called chancellors) who similarly gave time to ensure covering all the legal bases.

Beginning with the expansion of awareness and the sharp increase in legal problems related to sexual abuse, local congregations and judicatories have found themselves in new territory. The "volunteer" lawyers often do not have the experience with or competence in the complex issues in sexual abuse. A new breed of litigators has appeared, both for victims of abuse and for perpetrators. A minefield of legal complications surrounds each case, and the costs of following bad advice can be enormous.

One presbytery executive I trust told me what it felt like from her office: "Last year we had nine cases we worked on at one time or another. They were enormously time consuming. We did not have to go to court on all of them, but we had to have the very best representation we could get." I asked how much money it had cost, and she said $90,000. "Where did you get the money to pay for it?"

"We were lucky," she said. "I had a reserve fund of $40,000, and church insurance sources came up with the other $50,000." She continued, "But now my reserve is gone. I don't know what I'll do next year."

When I talk about litigation costs as an unexploded bomb, I'm referring to the rapidly increasing cost of specialized legal representation. In our society, organizations such as churches and judicatories are increasingly likely to be involved in complex legal issues—sexual abuse, zoning, landmarked buildings, personal injury. In many cases the pro bono legal help we used to count on will not cover what is needed. Those costs can be substantial.[14]

I note the obvious, too. Some of the celebrated sexual abuse cases have resulted in large judgments against groups in the churches. Sexual abuse judgments have escalated sharply, with the first hundred million dollar judgment level having been hit in 1997. The pressure of those payments is usually covered by insurance, but the consequent rise in insurance costs is significant.

Summary

In the previous chapters I let the cat out of the bag about the serious condition we are in because of our finances. In this chapter I have been trying to explore threatening signs of possible problems that have yet to become fully visible. If they do move from potential to actual threat, some of them could have severe impact very quickly.

I have identified these potential trouble spots as funding glitches, entitlements, and unexploded bombs. All of them are already affecting some of the churches. I hold them up as warnings, with every hope that none becomes as hurtful as any of them can be.

But basic questions remain: Why have we in the churches not been more responsible in dealing with these financial issues? Why have we not demanded that our leaders address them openly and clearly? Why have we, who teach the responsibility of stewardship in all our congregations, been so remiss as stewards of the institutional resources we have been given? These questions echo the question in the first chapter of this book: Why do the churches make such short-sighted and inadequate plans for dealing with financial matters? Why do we seem to hide from the truth of our situation? Why do we choose leaders who will not communicate clearly what the situation is? Why do we appear to collude with each other in a conspiracy of silence about church finances?

Let me summarize what I have been saying about the leadership we have given or given our assent to. On our watch, I believe the following is happening:

> **We are spending our current income and our savings as if there were no tomorrow.**
> **We are making promises we most likely will not to be able to keep to people and to programs.**
> **We are making commitments to organizational models for the future in spite of the fact that they are not working today.**
> **We are postponing problems for tomorrow with no plans for making tomorrow's resources adequate for dealing with them.**
> **We are spending our institutional capital to pay current bills.**
> **We are counting on tomorrow's churches to be able to deal with larger problems than those we have; even so, we are using up the resources they will need.**

Meltdown is the metaphor I am using to describe the destructive nature of the financial condition into which we who are church leaders have led this great institution. It may be an even better metaphor for what is happening to the leadership of the churches in trying to deal with this financial condition.

CHAPTER 4

How Did We Get Here?

In this chapter I invite you into a different mode of thinking—analogical more than rational, making use of the other side of the mind. Thus far I have been addressing issues in linear, rational argument, although you can see in my asides and footnotes that there is another side to my thinking.

Now I want you to take a quick, light look at some historical movements in the political and economic worlds. In each of these arenas, people caught up in building a future experienced real success at first and expected further fulfillment as the future opened up before them. In each, however, the early promise went astray, the world changed, and the promised future fell apart.

Obviously I see some connections between these worlds and the financial and institutional realities of the churches. I will try to stir your imagination and lead you to think more penetrating thoughts about our churches. These are evocative exercises, not exercises in precise history or economics. If it works, you may discover things that are beyond what I know. It is an invitation to your imagination.

At the end of the chapter I will share some of what the stories evoke in me, but the most important result is what they evoke in you. What elements of your own system are illuminated by reflecting on these scenarios that hint at parallels of how the church got where it is today?

Analogy 1: Iron Curtain Society

A decade after the fall of the Berlin Wall, Americans still find it difficult to think clearly about the whole society with which we had a cold war.

The Wall itself had become an image of a distant and threatening world. The Wall represented an ideology foreign to us. It seemed that Winston Churchill was right in describing that menace as an Iron Curtain. Both the Wall and the Iron Curtain became symbols of an adversarial world, one that was both secretive and threatening.

The symbols focused the suspicion and anxiety Western democracies felt about military and political pressures from the U.S.S.R. and Eastern Europe. Nearly half a century of angry rhetoric and political posturing about who was most "hawkish" and least "soft" on communism left us with little knowledge of what was actually going on in Iron Curtain society. Our ignorance probably led us to serious mistakes and cost us vast amounts in overspending for perceived "gaps" in defense.

What we regarded as a monolithic, totalitarian society, intent upon world domination, we are only now beginning to discover was actually something far more complex. But it took the fall of the Berlin Wall to dramatize that change. Think about the times just before the collapse of the Berlin Wall—the 1970s and '80s. The public impression was of a powerful set of enemies, ready at any moment to threaten anyone anywhere in the world. The U.S. made decisions about Vietnam and Cuba and Central and South America based on that public sense of power and threat.

But by that time the communist system was held in place by force and intimidation, not by popular support. To some extent that had been true for generations. But remember that the dream at the heart of that world was not force and intimidation. It was, rather, a powerful, almost religious, sense of hope for a society that was more just and humane than the one Karl Marx found in nineteenth-century Western European industrial nations. From very early on, there was intimidation and violence to support the dream. Nevertheless, a powerful ideological dream won the hearts of many people—at least in the beginning.

It is no small thing to dream of a society in which people are treated with justice and are given equal opportunities. The rhetoric of the Declaration of Independence embraces just such a dream, and that rhetoric, too, has been revolutionary in its time. It still is. One should not be surprised that such a dream had power to capture the hearts of many in Eastern Europe and Asia, even though repressive regimes quickly took over to manage the dream.

For people who had never known democracy or stability, building on such a dream must have seemed worth a try, worth sacrifice. The elite cadre that took leadership had an opportunity to build toward that dream. For those who believed in the dream, the early battles might have seemed as heroic as the Continental Army at Valley Forge. But the elite cadre of leaders did not build the dream. Instead, they built systems that protected themselves and gave the people only enough to keep them under control. They built systems that repressed dissent.

How did they pay for their system? With tax payments and a reduced standard of living. As long as the people believed in the dream, both made sense. As the dream faded, it was harder and harder to justify paying for a system that did not give you much of what you thought it was designed to give you. But the elites could continue doing what they thought best because there was a steady source of income that paid even for the repression of dissent. As the dream failed, the elite replaced the dream with fear of the enemy—the West.

When did the dream of a better society die among the people of Eastern Europe? It probably died in people one by one, as they discovered that governments were not delivering the kind of world they had promised. Many kept working for the regimes and for the reformation of the regimes long after others had given up. Finally the dream was nothing but rhetoric, and even the people who used the rhetoric knew it was not true. It simply bolstered the power of the elites who kept saying, "Trust us. The new society is just around the corner. We have to overcome our enemies first, then we will turn our energy to building that better society." Because they had the power to coerce the taxes and repress opposition, they continued to rule as they had in the past. The wall that seemed to threaten us was actually an effort to coerce those who had lost hope in the dream of a better future. It was to keep the people from running away from the land of broken dreams.

Fewer and fewer believed. Finally, the dream was an illusion. In the West, the symbol of the Wall stood for a strong, antagonistic society. Few of us realized that nobody was holding it up from the other side. It was not overthrown; it fell because nobody believed in it any more. Or nobody believed in the dream that had given it its substance.

As the emperor paraded down the street in the fine clothes his tailors had made for him, a little child said, "The emperor has no clothes!" And behold what the child said was true.

And behold, the Wall fell.

There were efforts to preserve parts of the dream. Mikhail Gorbachev tried to hold the disintegrating world together, but the time was too late. One of the great empires of the history of the world began to unwind, faster and faster. Boris Yeltsin became leader of the country of Russia, not of an international empire.

Could the same happen to our churches? Could their dreams go unfulfilled because they failed to heed small signs of dissatisfaction and lack of attention to seemingly routine financial matters?

This comparison is an uncomfortable one when I use it to think about the churches I know. It may be an unfair analogy. Perhaps the only learnings from it are caricatures. Nevertheless, I lay out the story, wondering if there may be some lessons to be gained as we think about what has been happening in our denominational systems.

Analogy 2: Industrial Giants

I turn now to a movement—the rise of great industrial corporations—that took place earlier in this century in another part of the world. Let me sketch thumbnail oversimplifications of three such cases.

General Motors

From the thirties to the sixties, the General Motors Corporation grew into an industrial colossus such as the world had never seen. The North American passion for automobiles, along with General Motors' imaginative multicar organization, generated profits and influence. It seemed the corporation could sell anything they could build. It became the economic engine for whole states and lifted personal incomes (not without some battles) across the country. When General Motors' president, Charles Erwin Wilson, became the U.S. secretary of defense in 1953, he quickly told us, "What's good for General Motors is good for America." His comment was a symbol of much thinking during the Eisenhower years.

From 1945 through the sixties, money flowed into the company just as predictably as taxes flow into the coffers of the state. The managerial elite, made confident by their years of success, assumed they knew what was best for the consumer. They ran the company according to their perceptions. They rewarded themselves generously with bonuses from the limitless flow of income. It all worked pretty well until the mid-sixties, when a new set of companies introduced automobiles that were more durable, more fitted to the customers' changing needs. GM management responded by doing harder the very things that had caused them to be successful in the first place: building larger, gaudier gas guzzlers, convinced that what was best and most profitable for the company was what was best for the public. They did not feel a need to take into account the fact that the market environment had changed.

In essence, the very success they had had earlier became the source of their failure to adapt. Then General Motors gradually discovered that it had to change or die. The flow of income from sales could no longer support the kind of institution it had become. The result? Radical downsizing, cutting out many levels of management. A new focus on what the consumer wants. A consolidation of operations. A focus on total quality management. Many workers and many managers lost their jobs.

International Business Machines (IBM)

"Big Blue" was the magic story of the fifties, sixties, and seventies. IBM developed its line of mainframe computers at a time and on a scale that no one had imagined. Across the world they became the benchmark for the new computer age. IBM, too, seemed to be able to sell anything they built, and sales fueled geometric growth of the company. They built a proud heritage of commitment to employees, being willing to transfer them, train them, or occasionally offer them generous packages for early retirement, but never, never downsizing. Management was confident that it knew what the public needed and wanted; they knew how to build it, deliver it, and maintain it. Money poured in to support all they wanted to do. Again, it seemed as steady as taxes!

But the situation changed. The future of computing switched to desk-top computers, not mainframes. IBM saw the change too late and then stumbled when it tried to adapt. Protecting an outdated operating system, the company wrote a contract for software that practically gave away the store to Microsoft. Hard times came. The company had to do the unthinkable: downsize—and again and again. Middle managers were released. With a smile, some observers say the ultimate sign of change was the loosened dress code. You can no longer identify an IBM executive as a white male in a blue suit and white shirt!

The assured flow of revenue generated by products stopped being assured.

The stock market (the ultimate arbiter of such matters) tells us that both General Motors and IBM may have succeeded in turning themselves around. But it took years of frantic work, investment of billions of dollars, and staggering personal losses.

The American Telephone and Telegraph Company (AT&T)

The third example is Ma Bell, that ubiquitous figure that dominated communications in this country during the first half of the century.[1] The government gave AT&T exclusive rights to the telecommunications business in return for their investing the capital for a distribution system that was genuinely national.[2] The size of the company was staggering. Everyone who had a telephone was a customer. Service was of high quality and you could count on it. Telephone employees called the company "Ma," because she took care of them. Layoffs were rare. Because the service was mandated by the government, income was predictable, down to the percent profit that the company could make. It was an industrial giant with steady income.

As the technology grew, however, MCI, Sprint, and then other companies discovered that they could provide a less expensive product. They sued the government for the right to provide services in competition with AT&T. Meanwhile the government itself began to question the lack of competition in this explosively growing area and brought court cases that resulted in breaking AT&T into regional Baby Bells. A large, powerful, effective corporation found the rules changed, and it has been scrambling, as have the Baby Bells, MCI, Sprint, and a myriad of new players.

There have been vast changes. AT&T has experienced so many downsizings that employees no longer feel "Ma's" protection. The flow of income that was once so strong and predictable now depends on individual decisions by customers. AT&T no longer owns the playing field. As far as getting telephone service, nearly every night at supper-time I get a telemarketer call from some telephone company. Ma Bell is reduced (and it does seem that *reduced* is the right word) to bribing me with a hundred dollar check to come home to her services. Ma, I'm embarrassed for you! As for me? I have all kinds of phoning options and I think I am getting a good deal, but . . . I don't know whom to call when something goes wrong. Something in me longs for Ma to come back and for all those others to disappear! Or at least not to phone at suppertime.

Some Reflections

We have looked at two kinds of institutional phenomena of the past few decades, political and corporate. Let me be clear: Nothing in any of these analogies directly fits what has happened in the churches. But I believe that all bear hints or suggestions that might help us think about what I have called meltdown. We are not going for precision here. We are trying to expose ourselves to some different situations and then muse a bit, wander a bit.

Historical and Cultural Context

None of the above scenarios happened in a vacuum. The Marxist revolutions grew out of the dislocations of World War I and the depressed economic and political systems of Eastern Europe. The growth of the American industrial giants was connected to a war effort (both the hot war of 1939-45 and the cold one of 1946-89), and to general economic and social conditions in the country and world.

This suggests to me that the churches' growth in strength and influence after World War II was not simply a condition of their inner gifts but was somehow related to what was going on in the world around them. The baby boom and the growth of home ownership in the suburbs had something to so with the rapid growth of many churches in the fifties and sixties. The growth of a strong middle class and a management elite in society had an impact upon the churches.

This period coincided with an age of apparent success among many of the dominant denominations of our society—if you define success in terms of institutional growth and vigor. After the War, denominations were not very committed to overcoming classism or racism, to facing sexism or poverty or any other demonic "isms" of that time. Those were blind spots for most in the denominations, as well as for denominational leaders. Some prophets saw those issues and took courageous steps, but most of the sense of success was really about members, money, and program growth. This time was also when systematic financial giving became an established reality in the denominations. As institutional entities, the denominations, particularly in the "mainline," found themselves popular, growing in numbers and resources, confident of their identity and their mission, and thoroughly bullish on their futures. They were on a roll!

Churches were increasingly filled with loyal, committed, generous members. They had modes of worship and community life that provided spiritual nurture that worked for many, sustaining them all the day long and through the shadows of the evening. Younger generations were led into their tradition and faith, and they moved into leadership roles as they aged. The flow of resources outstripped income of the churches in former generations, and the flow steadily increased.

Ideological or Technological Innovation

In each of my examples earlier in the chapter, "movement" was driven by extraordinary inventions of ideas or structures or technologies. Institutional vigor grew out of the conditions of the time, yes; but each was also a response to important ideas or technologies that grew to maturity in that time.

The ideas of Karl Marx, integrated with the power politics of Lenin and Stalin, made for the invention of a world empire of broad reach. That empire's ability to control dissent and to enforce a legal and economic system undergirded the costs of the empire and the political and bureaucratic elites who ran the society.

General Motors' extraordinary management system, invented by Alfred P. Sloan, integrated the production and marketing of a good product and made GM the giant it became. The unprecedented success of GM's marketing produced the flow of income that made the company flourish.

The sheer size of AT&T and the growing American demand for telephone communications, coupled with the innovations of the Bell Laboratories, made AT&T a colossus. The government mandated mono-

poly over the national communications network made for a captive
market and fueled the growth of the industry.

The invention and growth of the computer, driven partly by pressures of the cold war, put IBM at the center of the worldwide explosion
in industrial and scientific information processing. For many years, IBM
was the only game in town, and its profits from worldwide sales and
leasing furnished the resources for the remarkable growth of the corporation.

Less visibly, a quiet revolution occurred in the churches in this same
time period.[3] In the early years of the twentieth century, the concept of
stewardship became the innovation that changed the ground rules for the
life of religious institutions. The denominations used this new concept as
a way to stimulate the generosity of church people. Systematic pledging
and tithing produced new funds to support the expansion of the institution and the reach of its ministries. Church support, which had been the
responsibility of the well-to-do member, became a mass movement.
Ordinary church members in large numbers accepted the responsibility
of making regular contributions to churches a normal part of their lives.
The assured and increasing flow of freely given funds from masses of
church people became a hallmark of religious life in America. With that
flow of resources, denominations added managerial staff to focus and
direct their far-flung mission purposes. That managerial class—mandated to develop denominational mission—in their passion for mission
sometimes had a vision that was not the same as that of many churches
members.

The Problem of Success

In each of my four scenarios, the early successes became the seeds of
downfall. Success meant growth in influence and in financial scope. In
each illustration successful people and their institutions settled into patterns of life and thinking that made it difficult to hear or accept viable
options for change. There were no plots to slamp out innovation; there
were no plans to avoid adaptation; but the success they were already
experiencing simply reinforced their confidence in what they were already doing. Their very success cut them off from information about
what was not working. Success made them resistant to change. It made

them see bad news, not as indication that change was needed, but as warning that they were not doing the old thing hard enough.[4] My four analogies, each in its own way, illustrate the fact that, at a certain point, to survive, change has to be fundamental and radical.

Almost all the restructuring plans I see in church bodies seem to assume that the current difficulties are temporary, usually the result of not having done what had been planned long enough, or hard enough. The language I hear is of "turn-around," "bottoming out," and "fine tuning," not of facing fundamentally new ways of conceiving what they are up to.

The Role of the Elite

Companies, nations, and churches that go through periods of growth and success build a group of leaders whose very talents lead to many of the successes. But the assurance of the continuing solidity of the financial base and the growth of the flow of income insulates those leaders from their marketplace.

We see this easily when we look at a corporation such as General Motors; the management group becomes confident of its ability to foresee market needs. They come to be sure that they *know* what the American public wants,[5] what is best for the customer. Their products reflect what the customers ought to want. A talented elite group—with good instincts and hunches—can get away with this for a while. But in time, as elites tend to drift from what the customer needs, the customer eventually rebels. Buys a Toyota instead of a Chevrolet. A Compaq, not an IBM. Switches to MCI.

Churches have an even more difficult path. Their elites get what amounts to a faith commitment to their vision of mission or ministry. Their attachment to that vision becomes strong and ideological. The elite can come to see themselves not only as the management group, but as the "elect" whose judgment is ordained and supported by God. This view is doubly so when it is supported by a steady flow of increasing income for which there is no need to answer to an electorate. In industrial analogies, managerial elites defend their world against criticism and their jobs against change. In political and religious systems, the elites do that, too, but they may *also* see the critic as the traitor or the heretic.

Changes do not happen without talented people in leadership roles.

But from the analogies I have presented, I see problematic patterns that leaders can be sucked into as they control and regulate toward their self-identified "best direction." This is complicated when the elites generate their own income from an unquestioning flow of resources.

The Role of the Customer

The customer is the one the enterprise seeks to serve, the one who often has a loyalty to the nation, the brand name, or to the enterprise; who genuinely cares about it. In terms of the churches, the "customer" is the ordinary member who seeks to grow in relationship to God and to become a better servant to the world.[6] A Buick customer really wants a good car, but if, like my father, he buys Buicks exclusively for forty years, he becomes something of a fanatical supporter of the brand and the company (even if he occasionally gets a lemon). Companies come to count on the goodwill of their customers. And so long as that goodwill is backed up by good products and service, the relationship flourishes, and the flow of income to the company continues unabated. Within communist societies, the customer is the ordinary citizen who maintains a genuine loyalty to the nation, a loyalty that does not die with the first mistakes of a regime, but holds on until hope of the better life has eroded.

But most Buick customers will reassess if another company comes out with a product that seems much better. And even happy AT&T customers think twice when they hear that someone else is offering the same service at a lower price.

When large groups of customers become disaffected, it is difficult to get them back. Sales people point out that it is much cheaper to get a new customer than to recover a lost customer.

When large groups defect, the flow of financial support is interrupted. In the world of products it is easy to see evidence of a drop in sales. You can count how many sales were made in a week or month and compare to earlier records. In churches and political systems the counting is harder. Sometimes people stay on the rolls long after they have ceased to be customers in any committed way. The interruptions of the income flow may be intermittent or undramatic.

When customers back away from new products or activities, the temptation of the elites is to assume that "they'll come around" in time.

The first response of the elite is to repackage the old product. The elites are the last to want to recognize the disaffection of the customer. Avoiding the message from the customer is easier if information about sales and money is presented in confused, ambiguous ways. Customers who find an unresponsive elite are likely to become frustrated and angry, and to look for another company, political party, or church.

Franchises

Some businesses, political bodies, and churches act as if they have the franchise for their product and that the business is regulated. That is, anybody who wants a car or a telephone or a computer has to go to the authorized dealer. Nobody else carries it.

At times, that attitude works pretty well. In the early days of the IBM typewriter, nobody else had a top-line typewriter. If you wanted to use one, you even had to put up with leasing it, locking you into other IBM equipment and service; the company would not sell it to you. The product seemed so superior; there was no other place to go for something nearly so good. Franchise worked. For years. Even when computers came along. Then somebody sold a "clone." And the game had changed.

For many years the established Christian denominations had the "faith franchise" in most communities. Indeed, sometimes denominations felt they had a particular franchise for "our kind of people." Each denomination had a sense of uniqueness in its heritage, and people did not lightly change from one to another. Beyond that, organized Christian congregations were generally understood to have a franchise to meet the spiritual and religious hungers of the community. If people wanted spiritual resources or contact with religion, they could get that only in a church. Public acceptance of the validity of the franchise was solid.

In my Iron Curtain and industrial illustrations, the ability of organizations to enforce franchises is long gone. In Russia there is no longer one authorized political party. Dozens of parties have proliferated. The market on telephonic service has been deregulated. There are so many telephone services today that most of us are simply market confused. A "better price" for comparable goods will override loyalty to a brand. Few North Americans will shop only for GM or even the Big Three autos. IBM's turnaround seems to have begun when the company came to see that it no longer had a captive market but had to compete with better products and services.

Half a century ago a community consensus supported the idea that churches had a franchise on religion. Not only that, each denomination had a fanchise in its own niche of the population. But that consensus is gone. If you are eager to connect with genuine religious experience, there are a lot of options. Many of those options are not churches. As a Canadian friend put it, "Churches today discover that every community has a religious smorgasbord all around."

I am proposing that in American society, religion, too, has been deregulated. The franchise American society gave the churches to handle religion is no longer operative.

Church is not the only religious game in town.

Trust

In all my analogies, trust existed at one time between managers and customers, the leaders and the led, the structures and the members. The more trust there was, the more the system worked for everybody. Most managers intend to produce good products and experiences for their customers, and customers expect it. Most customers who have been served well for a time will give the benefit of the doubt the first time or two they have a bad experience, sometimes even more. And some customers build up a deeply loyal trust, like my dad's to Buick. But eventually customers become disillusioned if whenever they encounter their political leaders—or their computer company or their church—they find out that what they want does not really matter. Customers will stand still and accept it sometimes when the leaders tell them that what they want is wrong, or that something else would be better for them. But in the long run, trust wears thin. Loyalty no longer feels compelling. This is particularly true when it seems that the resources committed to the company or the church or the taxes are being misused: the automobile company gives its executives outrageous bonuses, the political party reserves all the best houses and cars for political hacks; the church gives money to a cause that the members do not identify as serving the purposes the church is supposed to serve. A few such shocks, every one of which may be defensible from the point of view of the elite, and customers begin to withdraw their support. Add to that the possibility that you have been served up several lemons, and the customers head for the doors.

All of the management classes of the institutions in my analogies allowed trust to dissipate. Of the one political and three industrial illustrations I have used, only GM and IBM seem to be facing the radical nature of the changes required for a turnaround. I do not see in the churches as substantial an effort to face the loss of trust as I have seen in those industrial efforts.

The Interruption of the Income Flow

Crisis develops when income is interrupted. At that point the system can no longer pay for what it is doing. Its carefully planned spending for objectives is on track when suddenly it becomes clear that income is not flowing in fast enough to cover expenses. The longer the system goes on spending at the same level after income has dropped, the more catastrophic the crisis may be. Systems that continue too long will find that they must cut staff and operations to the bone, and even that may not keep them solvent if they have no reserves.

Program leaders are the hardest people to convince that there is an interruption to the income. They "know" that what they have been doing is the right thing, that their programs and products are the right ones. If they are in churches, they are likely to be convinced that what they have been doing is "God's will." The universal initial response of these leaders is to work harder, because they are convinced that everything will turn around shortly. So much of themselves is involved in the way things have been run that they cannot conceive that it no longer is what is needed.

Trust erodes before income drops. Wise leaders who listen to the customer can pay attention to signs of loss of trust. Sometimes they can act in time to forestall interruption of income, but in most cases I know of it takes a crisis for leaders to face the need for change.

In political systems, the call may be for the use of force. In management systems, boards may have to step in to overthrow unresponsive management. In churches there is a call to restore loyalty.

In the analogies I have noted, the crisis was so overwhelming that it could not be ignored. Leaders had to take drastic action. None of the situations I cite is out of the woods yet, although all of them are making genuine attempts to overcome the crisis caused by the interruption of the income flow. All of them recognized that what had happened was a life-or-death crisis. Going on as they had been going, they could not have survived.

What bothers me is that the churches do not seem to be treating this situation as seriously as their secular cousins.

A Summary Reflection

In the first half of the twentieth century, the mainline churches built a religion "industry" the likes of which had never been seen before.[7] This happened at a time when other industries and institutions were being built, many of them massive, with enormous outreach and impact. The religion industry in this country captured a portion of the citizenry unmatched in any other nation. The industry was fueled by a remarkable innovation—widespread, systematic philanthropic giving for the purposes of the industry. Trust in the leadership and in the purposes of the industry soared.

By the middle of the century, even as the flow of giving continued to grow, the society in which the industry lived underwent great social and economic changes. Trust declined throughout the system as members' lives changed and values shifted, as gaps appeared between the commitments of the membership and the leaders. The pressures for change made committed leaders seem to act like elite groups trying to control the industry and convince the customers to be loyal to the products the elite knew to be best.

Facing the turn of the millennium, dozens of institutions reshaped their lives for the new American culture. The religion industry committed itself to attempting to do more efficiently the same functions it had been performing. It spoke of transformation, but, along with Canadian colleague, Stephen Hopkins, I wonder what category the transformation fits: resurrection, resuscitation, or taxidermy.[8]

CHAPTER 5

Doubletalk about a Double Problem

So far in this book I have been awkwardly straddling a gap, though it may not have been obvious to you. Most of what I have been talking about refers to a looming financial crisis. But I have also given hints and suggestions that deeper issues may be part of the picture. In the last chapter, I used new analogies to suggest a different perspective on the crisis. Many will find it a bit offensive to think of parallels between the church and a repressive political regime or a corporation. Again, note that my comparison is simply to underlying dynamics of growth and crisis. Seeing that dynamic working its way out in Eastern Europe and in American industry may help us to see—and accept—connections to what is going on in churches.

I do not think we can make sense of where we are in the financial crisis unless we begin to think outside the lines, using metaphor and analogy that help us embrace sometimes polar opposites as paradoxically true.

The imprecise language we use about church finances witnesses to our deep division, to the double-sidedness of this problem. I name the language problem, because church leaders and members rarely communicate clearly about the highly charged issues of money and finance. If we are, as I contend, facing perhaps unprecedented challenges in the next half century because of our financial condition, we must learn to talk straight to one another.

Two Issues

As I said, so far I have generally talked of financial issues, but the deeper issues are spiritual. Let me describe the two layers: (1) A severe money problem rapidly approaches. Our financial resources will make it impossible to continue the church's business as we have done in the past. Over the past century we have used up the surplus capital of the institution, and we are currently spending it much more rapidly than we are replenishing it. I believe this crisis will cause significant dislocations in church life within the next two decades. This is the financial problem. (2) The financial crisis we are approaching is part of a larger spiritual problem we have in America's churches: our inability to deal honestly with our own wealth. This is a spiritual and theological problem. I haven't addressed or explained this point directly, but I cover it later in the book. Keep reading.

I think we are doing a poor job on the first issue, because we have not been willing to face the second.

As I see it, we have no choice but to deal with both of these problems. Not sequentially, because we do not have time for that. Both issues are on our plates. We need to deal with them starting now.

In this chapter I look at our "financial language" and point out how our use—or lack of use—of words is laden with ambiguities, is less than straightforward, and is confusing issues, distorting our thinking and our actions.

In the subsequent two chapters, I lay out ways to address the financial and then the underlying spiritual issues.

In chapter 6 I give my best clues concerning what we need to do about the financial situation. This is a whole chapter of ideas and directions. Some I have already seen at work; others I see in planning stages; others I have discovered in conversations with wise church leaders. They represent the tip of the iceberg of possibilities.

Closer to my heart, though, is the material in chapter 7—where I do not pretend to be as clear. There I address the other question, the one that has been dormant in this book since chapter 1. What is going on in our hearts that has let us get so deeply in trouble, and what has kept us from doing something about it long before now?

This is dangerous business. I am separating our actions and planning from our deeper, more theological meanings. This separation does some violence to what I know to be true—that we really cannot separate our actions from our meanings.

Acknowledging the possibility of distortion, then, I owe an explanation of why I comb these two apart: in hopes that it will help us make better sense of what we must do and how we are to approach it.

Vocabulary Lesson

Before I get to that "combing out," I here walk through the financial vocabulary—the critical words—church leaders use. I think you will see that current church usage is so confusing and conflicting that little is communicated with any clarity. Let's look at the way we use some common words:

Money. In religious institutions this word is used with such ambivalence that church members cannot help but be confused. Do we love it or hate it? Is it a curse or a prayer?

Sometimes it seems to be perceived as a curse. Saint Paul said that *the love of money* is the root of all evil, but most people in the churches I know think he said *"money* is the root of all evil." This shifts the burden from the *person* who deals with money to money itself. That's a big shift, and it colors much church discussion about financial matters. If money *is* the problem, we should stay away from dealing with it. But if, as generations of church teachings assert (mirroring Jesus' words) the evil or good does not lie in things but in how *we use* them, we have very different concerns. Money, in this understanding, has potential for good *and* for evil. So long as we fear money, run away from responsibility, and practice lousy theology, we undercut our responsibility for wise use of resources.

Pastors are excoriated for preaching too much about money, because people want to avoid the subject and its hold on them. In fact, most pastors fear to preach about money and do so seldom and very reluctantly. Church members rebel against parish boards that cut popular activities out of the budget "simply because money is short this year." Although problems with money clearly cause many family breakdowns, few pastors or church counseling groups develop competence in helping people with budgeting concerns. Most church strategies for personal financial problems are limited to temporary handouts to transients. But if church members "fall short," everybody shuffles feet.

But in church circles money is also used as a prayer. There is an assumption that almost anything that goes wrong can be fixed if a bit of money can be found. A congregation that has isolated itself from its community and is slowly dying prays that another bequest or two will come through that will make it possible to struggle on in existence for a few more years. People of affluence in local congregations are treated as the local nobility and sometimes act like it, if they are not so put off by the way people relate to their wealth rather than to themselves. Pastors tend to have ambiguous relationships with wealthier parishioners because they feel intimidated by money.

Tithing, a word widely used in churches as a standard of personal responsibility for giving, generates equally disparate responses.[1] Some of those whose religious traditions have for generations taught tithing (by definition 10 percent of one's income) consider it a rule of membership. The Assemblies of God require tithing of members; many Baptist churches accept the standard but apply it less universally. Those who dislike any talk of tithing do so from strongly held positions: "It legislates giving." "It reflects an agrarian culture and a patriarchal religious establishment." "Why—when the government does so many things churches used to do?" For many the tithing standard triggers buttons about legalism. ("Before taxes? After taxes?") Some of the opposition reflects feelings that tithers act "holier than thou." (The tithers I know try assiduously to avoid such negatives.) One of the strongest of negative feelings is a passion for privacy about money. Tithing suggests to some people that a holy boundary is threatened—that "somebody" is going to "tell" me what I ought to do about money. Or, perhaps more frightening, someone is going to tell me I have to be responsive to others about what I do with money.

Proportional giving. This phrase became popular in several denominations in the fifties and sixties. The concept has since been taken up by the Independent Sector organization as the centerpiece of its effort to encourage giving to charitable causes: "Just Give 5." Independent Sector urges people to give 5 percent of their income to charitable causes and five hours a week of voluntary service.

Church proponents of proportional giving recognize their effort as an adaptation of 10 percent tithe; they encourage people to give 5 percent to the church, figuring the "other" 5 percent should or would go to other agencies. In short, it gives a rational answer to the legalistic conundrums that surround tithing, accepting the need for other charitable giving and also for the role of government in caring for those with needs. Advocates of tithing see proportional giving as a sell-out, as insufficiently rigorous, as a watering down of the "real" biblical standard. Many in the mainline denominations favor this system as more palatable than tithing, and a more realistic expectation. Quite a few see it as a strategy to get people to take the first step toward real tithing.

Endowment.[2] I know few words that strike such ambivalence in the hearts of religious leaders. The word, of course, refers to invested funds an institution holds in trust to support the institution or some of its programs for the indefinite future. For nearly two decades, now, I have been working with congregations that have endowments, some small and some massive. I can count on the fingers of one hand the number of congregations that were willing to talk directly about their endowments when we began in the mid-eighties. In most cases the endowments were treated like an embarrassing relative a family tries to ignore or keep safe but hidden away. As I work to get such congregations into conversation with one another about their special needs, problems, and opportunities, I find the most threatening issue has been whether or not they will "come out of the closet." Are they willing to "go public" with the fact that they have an endowment? Amazingly, congregational leadership often resists telling its own church membership about endowment funds. A few commonly heard sayings: "The only way to kill a church is to give it an endowment!" "A healthy church must live on the current pledging (tithing) of its current members; anything else is unconscionable!" "Endowments strangle a congregation's giving." Such comments are made with intense conviction. (*Kill, unconscionable, strangle*—we rarely use such strong words unless something is seriously disturbing us.) But the emotive statements and philosophical beliefs are rarely justified by real-life experience. Such emotion seems limited to the church community. One does not run into anything like that when talking to (even church-based) colleges and universities about their endowments. There, endowments seem to be matters of healthy pride, viewed with a sense of long-range responsibility. One does not run into anything like this with seminary endowments. One wonders if we can really be responsible about endowments in the midst of such pejorative conversation. Here we are clearly handicapped in dealing with the financial reality, because of our deep emotional reactions to the idea of endowments to congregations.

Planned giving. This phrase refers to a variety of tools and methods by which a person may distribute assets to people and institutions before or after death. The fact that tax laws make it possible for Americans to make careful plans for dispersal of their assets before and after their death, rather than leaving assets to the vague practices of state and federal tax offices, has opened up many options for people who make out wills, set up trusts, and seek to give their assets in perpetuity to beloved causes. Planned giving is coming late to the churches, with a growing awareness that a "windfall" of assets will be transferred by the current over-sixty generation. Denominational agendas will surely include this item more frequently over the next few decades.

Planned giving is intended to help people find creative options for dispersing their assets before or after they die—a relatively simple concept. Many people who love their colleges, local libraries, favorite charity, or local congregation may well want to include them in their distribution of assets. But around churches, I find that even talking about planned giving sets off seismic rumbles not unlike those set off by the word *endowment.* One would think it natural for a pastor, helping a parishioner who has a lifelong devotion to her congregation, to encourage her to reflect that lifelong commitment in her will. The language used about such encouragement, however, often reflects negative feelings: "grave robber," "opportunist," "blood-sucker." Clergy, having heard that kind of language, steer clear of what might be an opportunity to help parishioners be at peace before death. And parishioners, who have given weekly checks to their cherished churches, are denied opportunities to support the future of those churches.

Fund-raising. This phrase has a bad press in the churches. It seems too crass, too materialistic. We all know that we have to secure funds in order to do the church's work, but we do not like the idea of "raising funds."[3] We want to call it something else. Because we are involved with religious causes, we do not want to think of ourselves as using the techniques of secular fund raisers.

Of course some techniques of fund-raising may be inappropriate in some situations, but others can be of great help.[4] Many standard skills of a good fund raiser, if used in a congregation's pledging or tithing campaign, would improve the results of the congregation's effort. Fund raisers know about good record keeping, how to nurture contributors, how to prepare an asking package. Few congregations have much skill in those areas. Our ambivalence about money makes us suspicious of those who raise funds and cuts us off from helpful knowledge. Once again, our emotional aversions limit our possibilities.

Stewardship. I have saved a most sacred cow to discuss last.[5] This is a word everybody salutes. It is supposed to convey complex theological ideas about how we are given the things of this world in trust from God and therefore are called upon to return a share to God. This concept parallels the ecologist's suggestion that we have borrowed the world from our grandchildren and must take care to see that it is returned to them undamaged. Church leaders make every attempt to talk of stewardship in broad terms; just as we are expected to be good stewards of our resources, we are also engaged to make pledges of time and talent.

But in reality the word is perceived to be a euphemism for fundraising. This kind of doubletalk is genuinely confusing to many laypeople.

Everybody "knows" that the annual stewardship campaign is the campaign to get funds for the next year's operations. Everybody knows the stewardship Sunday is when the pastor will—usually reluctantly—give the pitch for larger pledges in the coming year. (I've noticed that evaluation of the stewardship sermon is usually how cleverly the pastor raised the *issue* of money without really talking *about* money.) Because most stewardship campaigns are held in the fall, everybody "knows" that any special program in October or November—a parish dinner, house meetings, a Bible study series, whatever its name or format—is about raising money.

(The stewardship drive often includes long pledge cards listing every possible church volunteer opportunity. People are encouraged to check off activities of interest. Here's what often happens: Church leaders—in attempts to downplay the financial side of stewardship—are left with extensive lists of people who want to do something. But the church has no machinery for connecting the volunteers with the activities. My universal advice to congregations is not to invite that kind of participation unless they are administratively staffed up to deal with it. People who volunteer and then do not get called often end up resentful. And the message of stewardship Sunday has been made clear: It really *is* about money.) In the meantime, all the talk and concern about recruiting volunteers undercuts the congregation's message about money.

Above, I noted that stewardship is "supposed" to convey complex theological ideas. But I see it as a simple "pay-back" theology. We pay God back for the good things God provides us with. I think of it as

Garden of Eden theology; what God might have expected of Adam from the crops raised in the Garden.

I yearn for a more complex and straight-talk theology of giving and of money that takes seriously the ambiguous character of my life, of my use of everything I have, and the straight-out sick way that I often relate to money and possessions as well as my whole life. Stewardship leaves out my sinfulness, my need for repentance, and the reality of the grace of God. I don't mind it as a simplistic theology, I just wish we had a theology of money and giving that had more substance.

My final point on stewardship comes from the scholarship of Robert Wood Lynn, a friend, colleague, and historian by training. Bob has done intensive work on patterns of church giving over the past several centuries in America. He discovered that church leaders, between 1870 and 1900, latched onto the word *stewardship* trying to get church members to become steady, regular supporters of mission endeavors. For several decades these leaders had discussed the need for "systematic philanthropy," for taking occasional givers to mission causes and motivating them to give regularly, not just occasionally. The intent was so that mission planners could make commitments and plans for the future. "Stewardship" caught on. It worked. It was designed to help churches raise money and it worked. In spades.

So the use of the word *in churches* originated as a fund-raising tool. But in recent decades, church leaders have been trying to tell us that stewardship is not about giving money to the church; it is about a relationship with God. The charade has not worked. We keep using the word *stewardship,* but everybody recognizes the DNA of the original idea, even though we have forgotten the history and how this came to be.

Conclusion

In our use and misuse of these words—*money, tithing, proportional giving, endowment, planned giving, fund raising, stewardship*—we are crippled in addressing our financial problem because of our ambivalence and complex emotional feelings. If, as I contend in this book, we are in deep water in the financial crisis that is rapidly approaching, this double-mindedness, and sometimes doubletalk, about money will handicap us in solving our financial problems almost as much as it already complicates our spiritual relationship to the world and to God.

CHAPTER 6

What, Then, Can We Do?

In this chapter I try to pinpoint some places at which the application of our energy and ideas gives promise of helping us overcome some of the looming financial problems we face. Most of the actions I suggest will not be easy, and some of them may not work. For now our focus is on finding handles we can grasp for.

First, Some Good News

It must be clear by now that I see many difficulties ahead as we try to address the financial crisis facing the churches. There is much resistance and much complacency. But, fortunately, I see more than signs of resistance and complacency in the church. I also see genuinely exciting evidence of another kind of leadership emerging.

Item: This book is one of many currently being written by church leaders—lay and ordained—who are learning to talk straight about the church and its financial crisis.

Item: More and more congregations are asking new questions about investments in bricks and mortar and assuring the resources needed to maintain them in the future. Planning efforts are including more hard work on financial analysis.

Item: Religious institutions are beginning to struggle with managerial concepts that focus on collaboration among leaders who have a broad concept of improving the quality of how people work and what they are

called on to do. In the United Methodist Church, Ezra Earl Jones is leading what is called a Quest for Quality.

Item: Many congregations are working to discover who their "customer"
is and what he or she is looking for in a religious community. (I think
especially of the Willow Creek model of the seeker-friendly church.)

Item: The revolution in collaborative leadership is influencing how lay
leaders and clergy hold one another accountable for improving congregational life and outreach. Continuing education programs in seminaries as
well as independent agencies are teaching teamwork leadership across
the country.

Item: Congregations are learning to explore the world outside themselves—with demographic and economic studies—yes, even with marketing skills. Many are learning to do demographic study.

Item: Congregations are learning that a voice that differs from the consensus is not necessarily the voice of the enemy, but may be opening
doors to new possibilities. Conflict management and polarity management such as have been pioneered at the Alban Institute are providing
tools for leaders.

Item: Congregations with endowments are coming out of the closet
seeking to work with others to develop stronger management and more
faithful stewardship of those resources. In two denominations—Episcopal and Presbyterian—coalitions of such congregations are consciously
working on those purposes. Similar coalitions are being considered in
other denominations and in regional groupings. Denominational foundations, led by the Presbyterian Foundation in Jeffersonville, Indiana, and
its president, Larry Carr, are beginning to provide expertise in planned
giving and endowment management of invested funds.

Item: Many people have decided that the time has come to stop hiding
our heads in the sand, hoping that things won't get worse, hoping that
things will blow over. Such people are stepping up to leadership and
helping others move out of defensive retreat and hopelessness. In regional judicatories, where the crisis is often felt first and most painfully,

I find dozens of executives and bishops leading serious efforts to rethink finance and relationships.

Item: More of our senior leaders are actually putting on the mantle of leadership for this time, recognizing that nobody rises to the occasion unless someone says there is an occasion worth rising to. Lack of trust in the commitment and faith of the troops is lifting, I believe, and leaders are more willing to issue challenges, not palliatives.

I can provide examples of each of the items I have noted above. Some of the cases represent isolated voices and fragile beginnings. It is my conviction that these forces are growing, but I cannot prove it.

In short, although the churches have many characteristics of complacency and "business as usual," I believe that the voice of the future church is to be found in those who are leaving complacency behind and are moving out toward God's call from the future.

Rebuilding Churches from the Ground Up

In previous work I have suggested a number of ideas for the survival of the future church.[1] We have all kinds of challenges ahead of us. Here and now, I will stay focused on the financial crisis. As I think about the financial crisis surrounding the structures of the churches, I see seven principles that we need to incorporate into our rebuilding process.

Principle 1: Self-Supporting Structures

Our local, judicatory, and denominational structures must be designed to be self-supporting from their beginnings.

We have developed a system of financing our religious structures that depends on an invisible and unaccountable flow of money through an elaborate set of subsidies, handouts, and payments. The system is so complex that it is often difficult to know where anyone stands or who is responsible for what. What's worse, it is almost impossible to find out. There is a feeling in the system that someone will always come and bail us out. The final responsibility is always somewhere else. Dependent relationships are the norm, with all the underground resentments that accompany any unhealthy dependence. We have encouraged a church of institutional beggars and institutional do-gooders. Non-self-supporting congregations are often subsidized by denominational structures or well-to-do congregations and learn to live on the dole. The behavior of the donors and of the recipients often mirrors the worst in the social welfare systems of our local government. Subsidies need to end—subsidies for any religious structures.

I do not mean to suggest that groups should not share resources to accomplish tasks jointly chosen, even when one partner disproportionately furnishes the sweat and the other the finances. Live partnerships between equals are to be affirmed; co-dependent relationships between givers and receivers are to be eliminated. Having worked for twenty-five years to help churches recognize the importance of mutual accountability through contracting for services, I affirm two things: (1) how difficult it is to change the dependent system, and (2) how much healthier it is to reach beyond dependence to accountability.

If a religious structure cannot generate enough resources to secure its own life and work, it must take full responsibility for its own deficit. The psychological climate of begging and handouts is dysfunctional and needs to be replaced by a climate of clear negotiation and accountability. The system currently operates as an "enabler" and rewarder of irresponsibility and poor behavior. Every religious institution needs to be subject to the "sunset law": that the organization should end when its function ceases to matter. No institutional structure within the church should be assumed to have a claim on permanence. We need to learn how to let die institutional structures that have completed their tasks and served for their time. We can celebrate their contribution without being black-mailed into mouth-to-mouth resuscitation. This goes for congregations, committees, judicatories, seminaries—and every denominational sacred cow.

Principle 2: Income and Expense in Clear Language

What the church receives and spends should be stated in plain language.

All members of a congregation ought to have access to clear and full statements of what things cost, where money comes from, and how it is spent. The statements need to be in a form that can be compared to those of previous years. The same principle applies at all levels of religious institutions. What are the costs to congregations of having a pastor? What are the costs to a presbytery of having a presbytery executive? How much of the pastor's time is allocated to denominational work, and what is the cost of that? How much of a bishop's time is spent in national meetings of bishops, and how much does that cost? How much does it cost for a judicatory staffperson to spend a day in a congregation? Where does that money come from, and who makes the decision for that day to be spent that way?

An added element is the need to develop financial systems and categories that are consistent from congregation to congregation within denominations as well as beginning to work on that relationship from denomination to denomination.

We need to build a consciousness that clarity in churches' financial dealings is important–a complex task in itself. Next we need to begin to name the many significant unspoken assumptions that guide us and recognize that those assumptions sometimes involve significant financial commitments (assumptions such as "Every congregation requires professional clergy leadership" and "Clergy need three years of training in a theological seminary"). In the long run, such consciousness might well cause us to question some of the ways we use our resources. As it is, most such decisions get made by the seat of the pants, by the "feel" of the issue, by "what we've always done around here," or by whatever an individual wants to do. If we had better and clearer conversation about these costs, we might well use our resources more responsibly.

Principle 3: Whole-System Restructuring

Restructuring must involve the whole system, not just the offices facing change.

Decisions about restructuring one level of the church should never be made without input from those in levels below and above the level under consideration. Church restructuring and reorganization must be done in a framework that is more than self-referencing. That is, the people in the system to be reorganized or reinvented are not the only people who need to be considered and consulted in the redevelopment effort. One must invite the "customer" into the conversation early on. The restructuring of the board and administration of a judicatory, for example, should not be done without strong, if not leading, input from the congregations that compose it, and even from people the congregations are called to serve. Congregations should not restructure themselves by paying attention only to the desires of the congregational leaders. They must listen to other congregations and to their judicatory. They must listen to the unchurched "customer." In each situation the specific course of action may be different, but the principle should stand: that restructuring never takes place without input and participation from important constituencies including the public customer—who has not traditionally been consulted. Among the "other levels" of the structure that need to be consulted, we must include the historic traditions and leadership patterns of the past. Sometimes old historic structural patterns provide an important bank of resources that bring perspective for response to immediate pressures. The historical experience of the denomination needs to be brought into tension with the immediate needs a congregation sees in its neighborhood.

Principle 4: Consultation Not Veto

People whose system is being changed should be consulted but should not have a veto.

Changes in church systems will significantly impact people, both clergy and lay, employed by the church. Changes in the world of theological education will significantly impact those who teach and administer in seminaries. Changes in the churches will impact those who hold positions in regional and national judicatories and in the agencies of the churches. Clergy, seminary professors and administrators, and judicatory executives and staff have inordinate power in the decisions churches are going to have to make to face the approaching financial crisis. The churches must find a way to hear the wisdom of their experienced leaders, but not be blocked from actions that may mean loss of power or professional security for those in leadership. Many professional positions may well become redundant in the next two decades, and the church will have to make decisions about downsizing (or "right sizing") that will mean career changes for many who now have positions of leadership.

Traditions as valuable as the "freehold" pastorate and tenure in academic or other positions may have to be drastically curtailed or ended.

Principle 5: Shared Financial Responsibility

We all have a financial responsibility for making right the mistakes of the past.

We must begin with the assumption that the people who made the institutional choices in the past made the best choices they knew how to make. Their number of rights versus wrongs is probably as good as or better than ours. But some of those mistakes—the overexpansion of theological seminaries after World War II, the standard that every congregation should have a full-time professional leader—have left us with problems that must be made right in the coming generation.

The church has been unwilling to admit how badly we have managed our institutional framework and how we have accumulated severe financial needs that far outstrip the giving standards of even this generous generation. We have been unwilling to state real costs. I know of no congregation that has a responsible program of setting aside funds for building depreciation. I know of no theological seminary that has adequate depreciation built into its program. It is as if we are afraid that telling the truth will be too much for people. Instead, we wait until the wolf is at the door and have a crisis capital campaign to do what we should have been doing all along. Meanwhile, we go on building buildings we made no provision to care for. It is as if we worry about wolves at the door, but meanwhile developing ways to multiply the wolf population.

We have fostered a way of thinking that leads every church member to expect a full-time professionally trained clergyperson, pulling all sorts of subsidies and subterfuges to cloud over the fact that congregations are increasingly unable to afford that style of living. We continue to foster an image of church that the overwhelming number of congregations do not and cannot pay for. We are unwilling to name the truth that more than 50 percent of our congregations are below subsistence level, burning up all their resources paying for current operation. Our strategy to get out of that fix seems to be to start new congregations (we call it planting) with the same built-in economic model that is already not working for the bulk of the congregations we have. Is it that we do not trust the people of the churches to do church within different models?

Mistakes have been made, and those mistakes are the responsibility of the whole church, not just of the people directly involved today or tomorrow. Many clergy, for example, were called to and prepared for full-time professional leadership in a church that can no longer afford to pay a full-time salary. That is not entirely the responsibility of the pastor squeezed out of a job. The larger church needs to invest in developing systems to redeploy such people, to support them in retraining, or whatever is needed; the cost should not be simply "their problem." The overbuilding of seminaries gives us a greater capacity for producing trained professional leaders than the "market" can use, but I argue that the whole church bears responsibility for helping seminaries discover new and productive leadership roles development within the denominations. And the congregations that were taught for generations to aspire to employ full-time professional clergy but can no longer afford it need support in unlearning one model of ministry and engaging with another. The point in all these cases is the same. The church must assume as a whole the pain of those parts displaced in the rebuilding. Let me be even more direct: Undoing those mistakes will cost money, and I do not think it is fair to put the entire cost on the people who in good faith did what they thought the church was asking them to do. These costs will not be light.

Principle 6: Endowments Out of the Closet

Endowments and the use of endowments must come into the open.

Most church leaders and institutions are secretive about what their endowments are and how they are used. The financial portion of a church's endowment needs to be fully public. There is no place for hiding resources, partly because the effort seems aimed at hiding ourselves from the responsibility of managing such resources. There needs to be a strong dialogue among congregations and denominations about the use of such resources, and secretiveness muddies the discussion and makes us irresponsible in our managing and using them.

Appendix A is a set of Guidelines for Endowed Congregations developed in a workshop of the Presbyterian Network of Endowed Congregations in 1987. Participants in that workshop were surprised at how elementary and basic the guidelines needed to be. There was consensus that many congregations had given almost no thought to even these basic issues.

Principle 7: Balanced Bottom Line

The bottom line must be kept balanced.

The church as an institution must organize its life to live within its means. The purpose of this book is to confront the fuzzy organizational thinking that prompts the institution to plan budgets irresponsibly and then expect supernatural intervention to fix the mess. I have seen too many groups unable to make a responsible decision throw up their hands and say, "Let's just pass a regular budget and put all the extras in a 'faith' budget and pass that, too." These people often spend based on the faith budget without noticing that their income is at or below the level of the "regular budget." I do not want to question the need to make some pushes beyond where the budget seems to be. But even then, such steps should be taken only under very careful and circumscribed rules. Budgets must be real, must reflect real income and outgo, and losses in one year must be compensated for by surpluses in other years. Building maintenance costs need to be stated clearly and not treated as an "off the books" set of expenses. This is the bald fact that the churches have not lived by for the past half century. They have no choice for the future.

I suggest these principles as helpful directions to include in all our rebuilding. They are appropriate for the rebuilding we must do with congregational structures and for the reshaping of our judicatories. They provide guidance for how we approach the management of our seminaries and church-related colleges and universities. I am calling for straight talk, accountable relationships, and open dealing with the financial underpinnings of the churches. This is not what we have now.

But there are initiatives we must begin to take even before we have all our principles fully in place, before our ducks are in a row. Let us move to some of them.

Initial Initiatives to Address Meltdown

The immediate challenges before us are daunting. Here I lay out some challenging questions. The common factor in all five of these issues is their immediacy. These questions are on our agenda today.

1. A major portion of the churches' income is contributed by older donors whose generosity will not be available much longer.[2] How will we replace those gifts? How long do we have?
2. The tasks of rebuilding, inventing new structural systems, and re-organizing require some new short-term funds. Turnarounds cost money. Where do we get the resources for the experimentation, the research and development on new styles of doing church?
3. Many clergy will be squeezed out of full-time jobs over the next few decades as small congregations are pushed to the wall. How will we support them in their transitions to new careers? What will be the new costs?
4. Congregations moving from full-time pastors to a shared pastors will experience a difficult transition, one the judicatories have not helped with very much in the past. Some congregations may need to be closed and others merged. The church's available how-to help is virtually nonexistent. We will need resources for helping those many congregations with difficult passages. How can we make each of those passages a movement to a more creative stage of ministry? How will we fund such efforts?
5. The total cost of the delayed maintenance on the church's physical plant is enormous. What is our responsibility for the costs of the large, land-marked historic buildings? Where do we get the funds to do the essential repairs to that infrastructure? What new processes do we need to help us determine what is essential?

These are the challenges on our plates today and in the immediate future. Considering them, I propose these turn-around initiatives to survival and health. I believe we can begin working on them now.

Challenging Aging Donors

We must take a serious new look at the giving of our senior generation.

For new funds we must *first* look to the very people who are our major donors now. Although they have given much, we must expect more of them. The people who are pledging and tithing today are the ones we must count on for the bulk of the new funds we need to finance transition.

I think it is time to come clean. The institutional apparatus that the churches have accepted as normative costs substantially more than the churches' income. Since the churches' rapid expansion after World War II, they have built a framework that depends on continuing geometric increases of income and membership. Neither of those increases has occurred, but the churches have not faced the facts.

The parents of the baby boom have been aptly called the builder generation. They were raised to be "savers," to be aware of the future. Even now, they have the interest and the resources to help begin the turnaround. I believe they can and will rise to the challenge, if the churches come clean about the need for reform to guarantee a viable church for their great-grandchildren and start seriously working at that reform. Yes, sucn people may be resistant to change, but they want to leave an honorable legacy.

What is needed? Operating expenses, yes, and funds to make critical changes in these neglected areas:

1. Radical downsizing of professional staffs everywhere—in congregations, judicatories, and national structures. As with any downsizing, there are up-front costs of discovering new ways of defining what work needs to be done and figuring out how to do much of it without professional staff; retraining and releasing of professional staff, helping them find challenging missional vocations not paid by the churches; "buying up" the contracts of those with tenure, and eliminating tenure in the future. The "savings" of this downsizing will not come right away. New funding will be needed.
2. Rethinking the church's investment in physical plant. Congregation by congregation, judicatory by judicatory, we must inventory our building supply and needs; discover where the plant is redundant; restore those parts of the plant that have deteriorated; come to terms with the meaning of land marking of historic buildings and set workable strategies about them; plan and carry out the capital campaigns called for to accomplish these aims; become more conservative about new building, biased against building anything that does not have a built-in endowment for building repair and maintenance. We will have to close and consolidate congregations to reflect demographic changes. We must convince fiercely independent congregations to work with one another on these delicate issues involving their own survival.

3. Reimagining the life of the local congregation to fit different situations. We will need to explore different scripts for congregations, going beyond "one size fits all" to a variety of congregational styles to fit different religious ecologies, ethnic patterns, and cultural settings. We need strategies to help existing congregations evolve into new kinds of worshipping and witnessing communities.

4. Clarifying the financial needs of new church arrangements and how to support them. Through a period of research and development, we must calculate the real costs of making these changes and then plan what it takes to maintain and support such a system of institutions.

These changes will cost money now to conserve money later. Judicatory and denominational leaders must take the lead in communicating these real needs to lay and clergy congregational leaders. This calls for a forthright honesty that the institutional leaders have shied away from. Lay leaders may discover that what they had thought to be sacrificial giving to their church will need to be doubled or tripled to undergird the change.

I challenge especially the senior generation to take the lead in serious theological exploration into a deeper and more comprehensive understanding of the relationship between possessions and redemption. (I will have more to say about this in the next chapter.)

If one thing is clear to me, it is that the current generation of seniors in our churches is essential to the future of the churches. They have a major contribution to make to the future of the churches they have had such a formative hand in developing. Although the time must come when this generation passes the baton to the next, I believe we must still depend upon them for major contributions. I believe they are up to it if they are challenged.

Developing Effective Education in Biblical Generosity

We must develop effective education in biblical generosity. We must have as a goal the raising up of new generations of benefactors as or more generous than as our current senior generation.

Churches are silent, on the whole, about money and wealth with two exceptions—during the few weeks before an annual campaign and at the time of special financial needs or crises. This must end. As Jesus used the topic of money and wealth as a staple of his teaching ministry, the church must return to regular, continuous confrontation of our culture's value of self-indulgence and the church's culturally based value of individualism and privacy about money. Pastors, particularly, must be asked to become the preachers, teachers, and leaders we need in relationship to money. That means they will need help to deal with their own fears and ambiguities in this area. Churches have been content to leave the issue of values to TV advertisers and have abdicated the field by their silence. That abdication must end.

Most education about being generous does not come from formal classes. Generosity is contagious—from person to person. We have in our churches an extraordinary cadre of laypeople who have lived generous lives—some more than others. But congregational life must be structured to foster one-on-one conversations about what it means to give. Financial campaigns that are carried out in the mails or on the phone certainly are "easier" than door-to-door campaigns, but they rarely lead to much growth in the giver or the asker. Door to door *is* difficult to organize, but that is not the only way to get one-on-one conversations going. Congregations need to bring about conversations to happen among adults—deep conversations about values, about the meaning of sacrifice, and the connection to what God is and does. People and their patterns of giving do not change much without that. Obviously I am talking about life-changing conversation, not simply sales pitches about meeting a budget. And such conversations may result not so much in people giving more to specific institutions (including the congregation) but in their becoming more generous in relationship to other community needs. The critical opportunity for the witness of the older generation to younger church members is clear. Perhaps our senior generation can undertake mentoring the young in generosity.

The church also has a critical stake in developing methods for people within households to delve deeper in discussions of values and commitments. We need to be building more generous relationships within families and living groups, not just building better church budgets. All congregations need to include conversations about money in new-member and marriage preparation or enhancement courses.

Churches say almost nothing to children about giving (to church or to anything else). Again, we leave the education in the hands of Saturday morning television cartoon advertisers. Then we wonder why children are captivated by the fad du jour. Are we then surprised that there is evidence that younger members of the church are less supportive of the church than their parents were? When were they offered a choice? What resources are there for helping parents and children explore issues of money and its meanings? I know of several mutual funds that provide educational kits for young investors, and I am using one of them with my four grandchildren.[3] And while churches are looking at teaching children about generosity, they would do well to use the gifts of the grandparent generationin this way, too. There is already a formidable alliance between of grandchildren and grandparents, which can be used to advantage. And how better, perhaps, to influence the thinking of the young parents—the very generation to whom the baton of leadership needs to be passed?

I note one more area under the broad category of "education": the potential for deep spiritual retreats about one's relationship to money, about the mix of selfishness and generosity that is in all of us. A good example of this is the work of the Ministry of Money, a mission group of the Church of the Saviour in Washington, D.C. This group pioneered Money Seminars that are held across the country.[4] We do need opportunities for more in-depth experiences for inviting God into our values, priorities, and decisions about our resources—not just into our hearts.

In short, we now need significant expansion of our education about money, wealth, and discipleship. Such a development will not have immediate impact on the impending crisis, but it will help change the face of our congregations in the future.

Facing the Dysfunctional Nature of Clergy Leadership about Money

Throughout this book I have noted the lack of clear, effective leadership by clergy in the area of financial management. Faced with financial tension in a religious organization, leaders tend to favor "spenders" over "savers." The tendency is not greed; it comes from their passionate concern for effective church programs of mission and outreach. But the task of a leader is to hold different poles of a tension together, not to side with one or the other.

I have noted clergy confusion about raising money or dealing with endowments. I have noted that congregations and judicatories too often lack strong leadership in setting up the conditions for effective financial controls. Conditions are allowed that make it possible for money to be misused or even embezzled.

In short, clergy are uncertain and uncomfortable about money, and their leadership in this area of responsibility is not as strong, clear, and effective as their leadership in many other areas. (Of course there are individual clergy who do not fit the stereotype, who understand their own relationship to money in all its power, who are able to minister to those same spiritual concerns among their people.)

Two changes are needed. First, clergy need a kind of education we do not yet have. A friend puts it this way: "Perhaps what we need is a new kind of therapy for clergy." In this area we badly need our clergy to be effective leaders; but they are not, on the whole, motivated to do things differently until a crisis arrives. Clergy do not need "head" knowledge but "heart" learning. They need to understand the emotional impact of money in their own lives and the lives of others. They need to know why they feel uncomfortable talking about money when Jesus talked about it more than any other topic else he is recorded as having talked about.

Second, we need laypeople who will be stronger church leaders in the spiritual issue of money and wealth. Many laypeople share the same hang-ups as their clergy; they complain about ministers preaching "too much" about money; they take public offense at any public accountability for financial matters. But laymen and women of great spiritual wisdom are out there, and they should be given opportunity to share their wealth of wisdom. Those gifted laypeople may need to become mentors for their clergy, mentors in dealing with the spiritual dimension of money, not in hiding from it. Clergy and laypeople collude in defining a diminished role for laity—"their job is to raise the budget." No. Their role is to call themselves, their clergy, and their congregations to spiritual maturity in living with money. Their more important role is spiritual leadership, not fund-raising.

I trust such a lay-clergy collaboration will help us begin to overcome the appalling thinness of our theological thinking about wealth and money.

Moving Planned Giving to Center

We need to move planned giving to the center of our thinking.

Although I will say more about this below with the issue of endowments, I address it as a separate category because I see such urgency in the matter. Since 1990, not-for-profit organizations have been falling all over each other to make their cases for inclusion in the wills of middle-class and wealthy North Americans.[5] Because all my children went to several schools and colleges, just as my wife and I did, I now receive mail from nineteen alumni associations. All are encouraging me to put that school in my planned giving. . . .

But the church is reluctant to put its needs forward and ask for bequests. The church must get off its duff on this issue. And the laity must not wait for the clergy. The fullness of time will be long gone before most clergy will have worked out their personal hesitance enough to be comfortable talking to people about planned giving. The churches have always had a few extraordinarily gifted clergy who saw the importance of challenging people to give for the future, and because of those few, congregations, seminaries, colleges, and judicatories were founded, and some now have endowments. Lay leaders need to step out and see that strong planned giving programs are in place across the churches. Any person who has ever made a gift to a congregation should be given an opportunity to make a gift to that congregation's future. Anyone who has ever pledged to a congregation ought to be personally invited to put the church in his planned giving agenda. Any Presbyterian or Catholic, any Baptist or Lutheran, any Episcopalian or Pentecostal layperson who cares for that tradition ought to be given a chance to vote in her will for the future of that tradition. It is not happening very widely now, often because clergy are too ambivalent to get out of the way.[6]

A number of groups of professional advisers have developed invaluable tools for planned giving. Financial planners, estate planners, lawyers, tax advisers can be a great help. But we do not yet have, and must discover, the personal, one-on-one models of exploring together our values and our desires for the world of the future. Through personal engagement we need to learn how the resources we have can make a difference in tomorrow's world and church.

Going for a Comprehensive Funding Strategy

Every congregation needs a comprehensive funding strategy.

Most congregations I know have in place a single strategy for generating funds.[7] At least once a year a major effort invites commitments to continuing giving (pledging or tithing). Or continuing low-key efforts encourage ongoing free-will offerings. The eye is basically on weekly or monthly receipts, receipts that are somehow related to the income of the people. Congregations prepare themselves to administer and carry out that strategy—usually depending on a volunteer cadre of members with little or no staff back-up. The effort is usually supported by a stewardship committee that comes out of the woodwork a few weeks before the annual campaign is to take place. Such campaigns usually just limp along from year to year. That such a haphazard system generates billions in gifts each year is astonishing. It makes churches the envy of all the other nonprofits. People *must* want to give to their churches if they give so much with so little encouragement!

I contend that this strategy is inadequate. Every congregation, no matter how large or small, needs a three-part strategy in operation all the time. Part 1: an annual campaign. Part 2: a periodic capital campaign. Part 3: a systematic, ongoing planned giving program. All of this, of course, is on top of a continuing program of generosity-education as outlined above.

Annual campaigns or efforts are basic. In most cases they need much more attention than they get. Better systems of record-keeping; the volunteers who do the work need more training and support; and each year's effort needs more planning and evaluation. In general such efforts are understaffed, because they are not considered to be as important as the "real" ministry work.

Every congregation also needs to realize that there are periodic needs for major investments of funds—sometimes for buildings; sometimes for building repairs; sometimes for special mission causes; sometimes for special opportunities. I do not know how often such capital funds drives should be scheduled—perhaps every five to seven years. The congregation needs to recognize this as a recurring issue, and not deal with it as a once-in-a-lifetime crisis. When winding down from one capital campaign, the congregation should be working very hard at nurturing the people who will be called upon again in five or seven years.

The records need to be organized to serve the future drive as well as the current one. The data from the annual fund and the periodic capital fund should be integrated and managed as one set of data.

Part 3 of the strategy is the planned-giving emphasis. Foundations established now need to be built on over the years. Lawyers and financial advisers in the congregation or the community need to be recruited to motivate and train members in long-term planning for their estates. Members need to be approached systematically in a way that is consistent with community mores.

Each leg of the strategy supports the other two legs. What is done in the annual campaign provides data and support for the capital campaigns. Every invitation to planned giving strengthens the church's case for regular support. A church with such a three-part strategy has also begun to put together a congregation-wide education in generosity.

Such a comprehensive strategy will not work without an equally ambitious leadership concern about the future of the community in which the congregation is located and the nature of the mission to which the congregation is called. Visions and plans are necessary, but so are careful analyses of what is going on and painstaking inventory of available resources. We must raise funds much better than we have in the past, but that fund-raising must be linked organically with internal congregational systems that are making responsible choices about use of resources even as they are sometimes making dramatic leaps in vision for the future.

Such developments require a new look at congregational staffing patterns. As I noted, most congregations do an inadequate job of staffing the annual financial campaign. We particularly neglect the work of affirming those who do make gifts, thus nurturing them for the future. We ask for funds much better than we thank donors.

In the long run, I hope many congregations will invest in staff to develop and carry out strategies such as these. Over time, such staffing should pay for itself, but not immediately. To begin, someone might underwrite such staff for two or three years on an experimental basis, or someone in the congregation with professional experience might be willing to be a development officer on a part-time or volunteer basis (or on a contract basis for "a dollar a year." Whatever the method, this must be treated as an important front-line role in the heart of the church's ministry—not just as "fund-raising."

Again, this is an area in which we can begin now.

Looking into Endowments

Endowments require much more research and development.

Having made the case that endowments are important, I also think churches have been poor stewards of endowments they have previously been given. Consider some of the problems I have heard about or seen in working with endowed congregations over the past two decades:

1. Gradually dying congregations that hold onto life by eating up their endowment, refusing to change their behavior to reach out beyond their boundaries or members. When the endowment is gone, the church dies, often leaving members bitter that "someone" did not come in to save them.
2. Congregations that used their endowments selfishly, for self-indulgent programming, sending choirs to Europe, sending staff on expensive sabbaticals, subsidizing incompetent pastoral leadership, throwing their money and weight around in denominational circles.
3. Congregations demonstrating unbelievable naiveté in allowing members to make decisions about the endowment when they stood personally or professionally to make substantial financial gains from the decisions.
4. Congregations where clergy or a subgroup undertook private projects that were kept hidden from the rest of the congregation and the denomination.
5. Cases in which the desires of the donor were not fully respected.

I also know of several cases in which I suspect that improper, if not illegal, actions were taken with inherited funds.

For every negative story, though, I know stories of imaginative giving, of trail-blazing efforts, of life-changing initiatives by congregations using the gifts of previous generations. If, as I believe, the moral dimension lies not in the endowments themselves but in the actions and commitments of those who guide the use of the endowments, I see an exciting challenge—that extraordinary gifts will lead us to extraordinary acts of imagination in our missional response to God's even greater generosity.

Which is why I believe the time is pregnant for those who have endowments and those who do not to work harder at the faithful use of endowments.

The Presbyterian Church (USA) and the Episcopal Church have coalitions of congregations that see their endowments as special opportunities to expand their horizons of mission.[8] They have banded together for all sorts of reasons—to learn from each other's mistakes, to cross-fertilize each other's experiences, to train themselves in new skills, to learn responsible management of large resources, and in some cases to collaborate on projects none could support individually. I see those coalitions as the front edge of the kind of research and development we need.

My fear? That we would build up larger and larger endowments to make a self-indulgent church more self-indulgent.

My hope? That the people of God might rise to the presence of new resources in such a way that vision and mission expand exponentially, attracting even more resources.

Nurturing Major Philanthropists

We have a responsibility to nurture major philanthropists.

From the very beginnings, the church has nurtured within people the impulse to giving, to generosity, to philanthropy. In some cases, philanthropists have been those with massive resources, and only some of their gifts have flowed through the churches; those philanthropists have funded institutions, colleges and universities, research laboratories, national organizations. The churches should take pride in the extraordinary and often wise generosity of the many philanthropists who learned their generosity sitting in the pew or talking to a dedicated fellow believer.

In recent generations a number of those philanthropists have made major contributions to the world and sometimes to the churches—people such as Eli Lilly of Indianapolis, Jessie Ball Dupont, Arthur Vining Davis, J. Howard Pew, John D. Rockefeller, the Mellons. Living philanthropists have already begun making an impact upon the world at large, and some such as John Templeton and Helen Walton have made a clear mark on the religious world.

An urgent task for the churches is to nurture members who have the capacity for such philanthropy. The church's task is to call them out to philanthropy—and not just for church purposes. Pastors and lay colleagues of potential and current philanthropists have a responsibility personally to demonstrate challenging examples of generosity as they present real visions of discipleship.

But many such philanthropists are not called to or inclined to make their major giving to or through the church. There is suspicion that religious leaders are not always as wise as the secular world in managing very large gifts. Until we get our house in better shape, we should welcome those who set up foundations or other means for managing their philanthropic work. I still hope the day will come when no one will make better use of endowments than religious organizations. I am particularly aware of the impact of Eli Lilly's benefactions to many causes across the country, including funding a lion's share of the research that has been conducted in religious organizations over the past three decades. Lilly was a dynamic, active layman in Indianapolis. My question is, "How many Eli Lillys are sitting in pews in churches across the country today?" Who is challenging them to great acts of philanthropy? That is something their pastors and other members of their congregations should be thinking about.

We can also be grateful to those church leaders who are setting up systems and denominational foundations through which large gifts and bequests can be held for the benefit of the benefactor's own congregation, judicatory, or other church agency. Most of the denominations have foundations or agencies that can provide legal assistance and financial advice to those who wish to allocate resources to the future church. Some community foundations make provision for handling bequests to church agencies.

I have a dream that someday someone will establish a national research and development foundation for religious bodies, able to provide a structure through which bequests can be professionally managed to enhance the work of churches across the country.

Conclusion

We are in a serious fix financially. I am sure of that. But we must not wring our hands in despair. There are actions to take beginning now. In one place or another churchpeople are working on most of the ideas I have described here. Not only that, many of these people and groups are linked and are teaching each other as they proceed. The financial crisis is real. There will be real consequences—people will lose jobs, important agencies will run out of money, many congregations will face closing, opportunities will be lost for lack of resources. But we are far from helpless.

We must now move on to another side of this issue. I have been talking about a financial crisis. But the crisis is much deeper. I have given some hints about the other dimension, but for the sake of clarity I have intentionally held back discussion of spiritual issues. I turn to that now. You see, I believe there is a more excellent way.

CHAPTER 7

The Heart of the Matter [1]

Most of the people I know who lead churches are conscientious, some of them to a fault, and many are among the wisest people I know. I am speaking about congregational board members. I am speaking about ordained clergy and those selected for regional and national leadership roles. There are some klutzes, of course, but on the whole they are a pretty able group—certainly as able a group as leaders of most other institutions in our country. As a matter of fact, many of those people lead other great institutions also.

Why, with leadership like that, have the churches come to the serious financial situation I have been describing? We cannot but wonder.

The more I have studied what is happening and how, the more I am perplexed. Church leaders seem not only to be missing important signals from the economy and their own statistics, they also seem to be intentionally closing their eyes. Denominations publish annual statistics about money and growth, but nobody seems even to look at what the reports say. We have developed our systems of rotating leadership so well that nobody stays in place long enough to experience a ten-year trend, much less the thirty- and forty-year periods required to understand some trends. Many denominational leaders I have known came into office with high hopes of turning things around. By the time they realized what was going on and how limited their power to change anything was, all too often they simply held on a year or two until retirement and turned the unresolved issues over to the new exec or president or bishop.

What disturbs me is what I see as patterns of avoidance of financial realities. And I trace the avoidance to an implicit theology that treats one part of creation—money—as evil. It is a theology that denies the sacramental potential in that one element of creation. Nobody says that explicitly, but we act as if that were our theology. That is our operational theology, which flies in the face of the biblical record and all our formal theologies. I believe that is where the big problem lies.

Our Feelings about Money

To approach that problem, I switch gears again, as I did in chapter 4 when I asked you to enter into an exploration of analogies. Here I engage you by asking you personal questions.

Are you rich?

Stop. Stay with that question. Really stop. Hold onto the question. Don't move on from it. Are you? Are you rich?

Now, how did that question make you feel? Did a part of you take offense? That may well be; I have broken the distance between us and stepped into your personal life. I am aware that I stepped over a forbidden boundary to ask you the question. We don't ask others such questions. Especially in church. Things like that are taboo. When we talk about money, we do it elliptically; we do it apologetically and indirectly. I violated all the rules.

Why? To help you look at that place inside you that responds to that question. That is a place that rarely sees the light of day, a hidden place where we store things we would rather not look at.

I have taken to using that question a lot—in public meetings. The public response is always the same; I can predict many of the individual reactions immediately.

There will be a murmur. A sort of collective, *"Wait a minute. What right has he to ask that?"* Then a few hands will go up, tentatively. Somebody will blurt out, "Compared to what?" If I hold the silence long enough, I'll start to get comments such as, "With my mortgage and tuition payments, I'm darned near broke!" Nervous laughter. There is always nervous laughter.

Why does that question turn us inside out? Why did it probably make you feel uncomfortable? In my group sessions everybody tells me that his or her first reaction was that I had stepped out of line. Some say it feels as if they had been punched in the gut.

If I were to ask, "Are you married?" or, "Do you like to play golf?" I would tap into very different emotions. And other personal questions—"Do you believe in God? Do you believe in universal salvation? Do you

believe in a personal devil? Do you believe you have been saved?"—
could lead to discussion and possibly to argument, but nobody would
feel I had mounted a sneak attack. In a post-Oprah world, I could probably come close to getting away with even more intrusive questions: "Do
you think women should have the option to have an abortion?" or, "Do
you think adultery is sometimes acceptable?"

In our society I don't think any of those other questions packs the
emotional punch of "Are you rich?" That's why I asked you to hold onto
the question for a while. To feel it rumble around in your insides. When I
do this in public, I hold people on the question as long as I can, so they
will feel the question search them out.

The simple question packs punch because in our society and in our
churches this is simply not a subject you can talk about. I'm always conscious that I've done something "naughty" when I ask it. People sometimes throw their discomfort onto me. They ask me to define what I
mean; they sometimes say "none of your business"; some people really
get angry with me. That may have been your response when you first
read my question, that is, *if you let the question speak to you.* You may
be angry with me now, because I have raised questions about why you
didn't stop to address the issue. Another response is nit-picking and
seeking definitions that will make you feel better ("compared to whom?")
or justify yourself ("Bill Gates is the rich one. I've got peanuts compared
to him.")

The usual audience response is denial. "Raise your hand if you are
rich." Most hands stay down, and only slowly and reluctantly, one by
one they go up. Some refuse to participate.

Objectively the question should be easy to answer. I have never
asked the question in any audience in which every person present is not
rich. Some are absurdly rich in comparison to 99 percent of those in the
world. And others, just by being Americans, are probably better off than
95 percent of the world's population. That is also true of anybody who
reads this book. The answer to the question is so simple. Why, then, does
it tie us up in knots?

You see, wealth is the natural condition of everybody who reads
this book. Indeed, it is the natural condition of all North Americans. I do
not mean to gloss over the fact that there are vast differences between
the very wealthy and those in our society who live in severe deprivation.
Those differences are great, and some of them are unconscionable. On

the whole, wealth is the condition we start with in church and in society; our society embraces wealth. Look at the world of advertising. We are the society of conspicuous consumption. We flaunt it. It is one of the greatest values our society lives by—the hope, the dream of wealth. The "good things" we are encouraged to want in our world are the rewards of being wealthy. It is probably our central value as a society.

Why do we work so hard to hide the fact that we are rich? Why hide it even from ourselves? Why does our wealth embarrass us? Why does it make us feel guilty? Apologetic? Perhaps even ashamed!

Somewhere deep inside us is a place that cannot come to terms with what it means to be what we are. That is a spiritual question, and it is the one spiritual question all Americans share. It may be the one that most threatens us. It seems to be one thing we want to hide from even ourselves. It is as if we are ashamed of being what we are, and that we cannot forgive ourselves. If that is so, it is inevitable that our strategies for giving will be based in our guilt.

Are We Addicted to Money?

I propose that Americans are addicted to money. It is something that owns and controls us and our emotions, not something that we own and control for our own purposes. An addict focuses attention and emotion and commitment on that to which he or she is addicted. The addictive material becomes larger than life. It takes over. It takes on power to shape one's life. The addictive material can seem to offer release from stress and tension. It can seem to offer salvation itself, for the time being.

I see patterns that seem like addictions to me:

What wealth we do have often fills us with feelings of discomfort—approaching shame. We hide the facts from ourselves (one reason, perhaps, why we resist making out wills and why many are constitutionally unable to establish or keep a budget).

Some of us stay perpetually anxious about money. Can I make it until next paycheck? Will I find a way to pay my next quarterly tax? So I've made it through thirty years on a shoestring; will the shoestring last another month? We frequently obsess on the unanswerable question: How much is enough? Where can I get more? For some the anxiety is pathological.

We want to have money; we want more money; we envy other

people's money; and yet we disdain the "rich" for having it. We buy lottery tickets and hope to win. We feel envy of the person who wins millions and then are secretly glad when we discover later how his or her life has gone to pot. We are not fully able to appreciate the wealth or success of others nor are we able to rejoice in their blessings. And yet we wish we had their "luck" or "good fortune." We treat the extremely rich like pop stars and celebrities, but in doing so we dehumanize them.

Most of us know some, if not all, of these symptoms. Such behavior and feelings are so common in us and in those around us that we forget that they are not very rational. In a world of incredible riches and re-sources, we focus on what we do not have. We develop scarcity thinking that assumes that if anyone else gets something, it is something taken away from what we could have.

Our society is familiar with addictions. We have a simple solution to addictions: "Just say no!" as Nancy Reagan told us. "Just say no" is what temperance leagues have always told us to say about alcohol. "Just say no" is part of what twelve-step programs tell us, but at least they give us support, knowing that few of us are able to handle genuine ad-dictions without help. "Just say no" doesn't work with our addiction to money.

A friend of mine taught me about addictions when he discovered that he was not just a compulsive eater, but a foodaholic. He had an uncontrollable addiction to food and was unable to break the addiction. That kind of addiction is not like an addiction to heroin or alcohol, though it is equally fatal. Food is something one cannot simply say no to! Saying no to food leads to death. One can neither walk away from food entirely nor give in to the addiction and let it control one's life. The task of living is to try to find a way between the extremes. My friend tells me of a conversation he had with an alcoholic who had been suc-cessful in staying dry. The alcoholic said, "Compared to you, I am lucky. I can put my tiger under lock and key and never let him out. You have to let your tiger out three times a day." Every time that compulsive eater has a meal, he has to control his addiction, his tiger. No easy answers, there. How, indeed, does one control the tiger of an addiction when one cannot lock it up behind bars?

We who are haunted by an addiction to things, to wealth, to money have that tiger of addiction sitting on our laps every time we watch television. When we pay our bills. When we go to a restaurant. When we sign a mortgage. When we try to figure how much to tip a taxi driver. When we think about our retirement plan. When the church asks us for a donation. It is all around us all the time. It never goes away, and it never lets go of us. And we never seem fully to tame it.

In our world, we must learn to live with the tiger without letting the tiger destroy us.

Because we and our world are so obsessed with this particular addiction to money, the church must help us learn how to live with it—to work through the inherent tensions we feel about our wealth. It is my thesis that the church systematically avoids that primary spiritual task. I believe that systematic avoidance may be at the root of our dramatically collapsing financial situation. I do not believe we will do much about the financial situation without beginning to address the deeper issues. Meanwhile, we play institutional Hide the Tiger.

Avoiding the Issue: "Hiding from the Tiger"

Let me point to some of the ways in which I believe we avoid the spiritual challenge, even as we pretend to be dealing with it.

The Demonization of Money

The working norm in most religious organizations is that money is evil. At best, it is a necessary evil. At worst, it seduces the church member and the church to put attention on secondary things. It is part of the "secular" (which means bad or less good) world that is opposed to the "sacred" world, where the things of God are.

In a congregation, it's as if the people who worry about budgets are less religious than the people who don't. The tension generated by this norm is acute, because everybody knows that the congregation depends on some generous donors who provide a significant percent of the budget. Such people are often valued for their gifts, but devalued for what they bring in their person, their ideas, their commitments. Our assumption: "Money people" on the board are not "spiritual people." "Money issues" are not "spiritual," but "ministry issues" are. The corollary: Paying attention to management of resources is not really important.

Clergy-Lay Collusion

Most congregations live with an unspoken rule: The clergy will not address personal spiritual issues about money. The clergy are allowed to talk—a *little*—about church budgets and contributions to the church; but everything else concerning money and people's personal dilemmas about it is off limits. The laity will respond by trying to make sure there is enough money to run the show. Lay leaders take responsibility for the finances of the church so that the pastor can be relieved to do the "important" ministry. Everybody knows there is nothing the pastor dislikes more than having to pay attention to finances. Some pastors make a virtue of being "above" all that concern for filthy lucre. Wherever pastors say anything about money, it is assumed that the subject is money for church budgets. Usually it is that and no more.

There may be other collusions: The endowment trustees may agree to subsidize the budget, as long as nobody asks too much about how and why they manage the endowment as they do. Sometimes there is collusion not to let the "ordinary" people of the church know what the financial situation really is. At times finance committees collude not to let the pastor or the board know what the situation really is. Things tend to be hidden. There are lots of secrets about money in congregations.

Clergy Abdication of Leadership Responsibility

Under the rubric that money is "secular" and that the pastor's work has to do with the "sacred," clergy have written a brief that permits them to avoid leadership in the financial management and leadership of the congregation. They have accepted a functioning job description that excludes any concern for what I contend is one of the dominant spiritual issues every parishioner has: how to deal with material resources. This means that clergy not only give little leadership to the financial life of the congregation, but also set up a climate that sets little value on the functions of financial management carried out by others. In the congregation and denomination, this explains the poor attention given to audits and financial statements, to contract obligations, and to paying attention to financial records.

In lives of individual church members, it means pastoral abdication of one of the most troubling dimensions of living in our society.

I must admit, however, that there is another side. From personal experience and from a lifetime of conversations, I must say that clergy are often placed in very difficult situations in relationship to money.

Over-Identification of the Institution with God's Purposes and Work

The institutional forms we have as churches grew up in specific times to respond to the needs and opportunities of those times. Institutional forms have always been intended to embody truths of God that are greater and more profound than the institutional forms themselves. Church people have always tried to hold onto God while being slightly agnostic about the structures of their churches. Over the last century in this country, our institutional forms grew rapidly within a society experiencing incredible economic growth. Church institutions also experienced new, effective methods of religious fund-raising. The simple fact is that the institutional forms grew in response to economic and organizational opportunities. Strong, vigorous institutions of all sorts developed in church life. Some of those church organizations grew far beyond what was essential. For most people, however, it was hard to see which parts of the growth were essential and which were not. The institutional arrangements came to be seen as that which God intended for all time. In the decades in which the growth of the church's income has flattened out and slid downward, leaders have been demoralized to have to cut back on institutions they have confused with God and God's purposes. Budget discussions pit the "faithful," who want to preserve programs and structures, against the "faithless," who see a need for cutbacks and radical changes in our institutional arrangements.

The Ways We Raise Our Money

In churches we rarely talk about "raising money." We sugarcoat what we are actually doing with language overlaid with theological concepts or biblical notions.

One thing an institution has to do is to raise the funds necessary to pay its bills. By not stating that clearly, we often confuse ourselves and others. That's the first and least important way we muddy the financial waters. Our not doing that clearly is one of the reasons I find myself talking about meltdown.

Second, we have our own vocabulary for giving, and it is overlaid with confusing meanings. We talk about contributions, tithes, stewardship, and gifts, but we load those terms up with emotional baggage of obligation. What we say does not reflect the emotional message we communicate. As a pastor acquaintance said after a particularly successful capital campaign, "Guilt will go a long way in this world." Although the language of thanksgiving for blessings is genuinely intended, a pastor's comment tips us off. It comes across as a ploy. The message heard is "Pay up if you want to be part of this community"; sometimes "Pay up—you'll feel better about your wealth."

Money—the need for it and our efforts to secure enough to keep the worship and ministry active—leads us directly into a theology of works. The church pledge or tithe becomes the substitutionary sacrifice that cleanses the rest of your checkbook and, inferentially, your life. A subsidiary theme is that even though money is "bad" (see above) you can be "okay" about what you have and however you use it— if you give the right amount or the right proportion to the church.

Outreach

I don't know anything that has become a more central idea in church finances than what we have named outreach. It refers to a congregation's obligation to provide financial assistance to those outside its walls, especially the poor or those otherwise hurting.

I feel congregations and denominations need to raise serious questions about the way the church handles this issue. There is a knee-jerk response here that needs to be questioned, although almost no one does so. In categorizing "outreach," we have again split money into good money and bad money. Good money is money we give away; bad money is money we spend on "ourselves." Outreach becomes a kind of new law by which a congregation justifies itself. If an "adequate" percentage of the budget is allocated for outreach, then the congregation has thereby achieved its righteousness.

As I understand church life, *everything a church does is supposed*

to be outreach. The worship is outreach. The parish education program
is outreach. Every activity of the congregation should be dedicated to
strengthening its members for outreach and supporting activities of outreach. The church's life and mission should be shot through every dollar
that comes into and goes out of a congregation.

Outreach as giving money away is sometimes dead right. Outreach
as giving money away is sometimes dead wrong; it can be an idol. It can
be our way of making ourselves feel better concerning our profound
anxiety and uncertainty about our wealth. It can be a way to hide from
the tiger.

Churches that adopt percentage goals for outreach have missed the
point. One hundred percent of a congregation's energy and resources
should be engaged in outreach, not 10 or 20 or even 50 percent. Percentages are used to allow us to measure our righteousness, if that is the
game we are in. (I don't think it is.) Once again, our use of dollars becomes a bargaining chip with God, a sign of our continuing efforts to
justify ourselves. Or at least our congregation!

We need greater sensitivity to the resources we have and the needs
to which we should direct them. At times that will mean giving it all
away; at other times it may mean spending it all on our own faith community. Neither choice saves us. The saving is somebody else's business,
no matter what we do with our budgets.

Living with the Tiger

All through this chapter I am struggling against years of ambiguous
language in churches I know, against my confusion about the challenge
to my own values. I speak as clearly as I can, although I do not yet see
with full clarity. I am ambivalent about much of what I am saying. I raise
questions for others about the practice of tithing, yet I believe in it, do it,
and have been enriched by it. I warn of the problems of outreach, but I
am proud of my congregation's strong programs of outreach. I do want
my pastor to help me deal with the spiritual dimension of my wealth, but
by heaven he'd better not meddle with my values!

I myself am hiding from the tiger of addiction to money. I am hiding even as I am making a plea for us to stop hiding. I believe that many
of our financial practices, our methods of getting and using financial

resources, are designed to keep us hiding from the fearsome power of the pull of wealth we all face every day.

We have been unable to find a way to forgive ourselves for what we are. We have and we control wealth. Some who read this book have more resources than Croesus at the height of his empire. There is something deep inside us that knows we are less than we ought to be in every way—but our powerlessness in the face of money takes the cake. It makes us guilty, anxious, rigid, unforgiving of others. It makes us envious of others and judgmental about them. How can we be released from this burden? Through better budgeting processes? Better fundraising? More generous contributions? Better outreach programs? More tithing?

In none of those ways can we deal with the spiritual dimension of our battle with the principality, the power we call money. We cannot set it right by ourselves. The answer for us has been that setting it right is not our business. Someone has already taken care of all that. We are not under condemnation even for the things we cannot forgive ourselves for (thank heaven for the line in John's epistle: "If our heart condemns us, God is greater than our heart"! [1 John 3:20].)

The beginning place, then, is repentance. Turning around. Turning away from our reliance upon ourselves and turning to God. All our elaborate schemes to show God how wise and foresighted we are are beside the point. Our desire to prove that we are in control of it all—useless.

Repentance can lead us to new actions. It can lead us to stop kidding ourselves that we are on top of it all. It can help us begin living into what's going on now, not hiding, not afraid that others will find us out.

Repentance can also help us start being truthful with one another. It wipes away the need for lies and makes it possible to talk straight, even about finances.

Repentance can also lead us to one another. The power of hiding is that it severs us from the very ties to others that can bring caring and forgiveness. We must begin in our congregations and in our families to open up the wounds life has inflicted on us in our relationship with things.

Summary

Strange. We begin with a financial crisis, and it leads us to a spiritual crisis. We begin with financial meltdown of our budgets out there, and we discover a spiritual meltdown in our personal lives. Perhaps the financial crisis is the door that may lead us to deal with the hunger we have to find our way home to God.

CHAPTER 8

Money and Churches: Crisis or Opportunity

The familiar forms of religious life that have comforted and supported generations of us in North America are facing an unprecedented financial challenge now and in the next generation. I have used the meltdown metaphor to indicate how serious I believe this crisis to be. I have shared my worry that church leadership does not seem to be preparing to deal with the crisis, and in many cases does not seem to be aware of its imminence. The rank and file congregational members are unaware of any real crisis as long as their own congregation's budget stays in balance or nearly so.

The crisis is real. The churches are already spending current income and savings more rapidly than money is coming in. We have made future commitments that are important to us –commitments we may have to abandon. We have locked ourselves into organizational models and programs that do not work today, but we are already replicating them for tomorrow. We are postponing problems we have now in the hope that things will be better in the future, but we are not doing much to change our future financial condition. We depend for the bulk of our income on a diminishing resource—older givers. In the midst of the current crisis, we can see signs of trends in society and its institutions that may well make the financial situation of the churches worse in the future. There are other potential threats over which we have little control; if any of them becomes an actuality, it will be an additional threat to our situation. Our key trained leaders—our clergy—have, by and large, opted out of engagement with the issue and offer little leadership.

Is the crisis real? Yes.

Is it getting worse? Yes.

Is this a case of meltdown that will simply destroy the known church completely? I do not know, but I hope not. I would not be writing this book if I did not believe that committed action by churchpeople might influence the future. I do not believe, however, that much of the churches' infrastructure will survive the next generation without severe changes.

Will that be a good thing or a bad thing? It depends. I have tried—in chapter 6—to point to some action we can and must take concerning financial meltdown. A subtheme of the entire book is another meltdown—one that touches our hearts and our values. That subtheme, addressed more directly in chapter 7, is that financial meltdown may be a symptom of a deeper challenge to each of us. It is a challenge of the demonic power of our relationship to money, a relationship that paralyzes us and victimizes us like an addiction. I do not believe one meltdown can be dealt with without addressing the other.

In Perspective

The basic value of our society is that the material world is all there is. This is the value that has been central to the Western world for at least a century and a half. This value drives our consumer economy. That value contradicts the central message of the churches. The Christian faith has always held that the material world is *not* all there is. The physical world is the medium within which the Spirit of God is at work. For a century and more, but more intensely for the past eighty-five years since the Russian Revolution, there has been a worldwide civil war about values. The communist world affirmed materialism to be a historical tension, a dialectic, driving inexorably through class struggle toward a classless and godless realm of peace, justice, and equality. The capitalist world affirmed a dynamic materialism that was driven by economic tension, where free markets and competition would result in a life of justice and plenty for all. Both agreed that the material world was all there is.

The communist enemy was atheistic. Capitalism, although indifferent to God, allowed those who cared about God to worship as they pleased. Seeing these as the two choices, the churches generally sided with the capitalists. The value system of the capitalists became the values by which the churches ordered their life. In the United States, the churches did so very successfully.

The fall of the communist regimes left capitalism triumphant, with the church following along behind, wagging its tail on the winning side. We had become the tame pets of a value system that affirmed the importance of materialism but saw no real presence of God infusing the material world. The churches were in the awkward position of accepting the cruelties of the market system. At least, however, this accommodation left the church free to worship a privatized God, secure with tax deductions. To deal with our guilt about the inequities of that economic system, we invented "outreach" and "social mission" as Band-Aids for the culture. Our critique has been too shallow. There is much more at stake.

Our difficulty arises from our inability to distinguish between a materialism that comes from the Incarnation (truly this material world *is* holy if God chose flesh and blood as the best way to show us God's very self) and a different kind of materialism that says this world is all there is. If the material world is all there is, then Madison Avenue is right. Whoever gets the most toys does win! Money is how we distinguish the righteous from the unrighteous. The stuff of the world is an end in itself and is not infused with Spirit nor does it point beyond itself to the purposes of God. There is no sacramental reality to human love and caring, to generosity and forgiveness.

Our own individual ambiguity about wealth is a sign of our own confusion about the values of the world around us. Our guilt about our paralyzing addiction will not let us go. Our games of playing at managing church resources and our games about giving funds to the church or to others are played out against our desire to make it right ourselves. Through the generations we have invented ways to make ourselves feel good, as if we could fix it all. We have called those ways indulgences, tithing, stewardship—you name it. We have done everything in our power to fix it ourselves, to establish our independence of God's loving mercy. It is that loving mercy we avoid at all costs. To accept it is to admit that mercy and justice and love and forgiveness are from above and not from our cleverness and our management.

The financial crisis in the churches is a wake-up call to a much bigger, deeper crisis of the soul of the churches and at the heart of society. The churches have no stake in the kind of materialism that capitalism stands for. Yet the churches' relationship to the material world, to wealth and to money, has become captive to the reductionist values of capitalism.

There is a spiritual call to the churches in the financial crisis. Can the churches again begin to conceive of what it means for the Spirit of God to infuse the very life and work of the people? Can we rediscover the power of God in the things of the world? Can we recapture the holiness of creation? Can the things we do in our churches and in our personal lives reflect into our society the holiness of all life and of all things? Can our money and our use of it reflect the grandeur of God's hopes for us? And of God's forgiveness of us—forgiveness even for being wealthy? Can we understand the very stuff of the world to be a sacrament of the kingdom of God?

I started my pilgrimage into the money problem of the churches reluctantly. I do not like to deal with money, and I am probably an incompetent manager of it. I started my explorations because I saw signs that tremendous, unacknowledged forces were buffeting the churches and the people I knew. I started my pilgrimage looking for better ways of understanding, and then of dealing with, the financial problems I saw all around me.

Is there financial meltdown in the churches? We may be closer than we think. But is there a more personal meltdown—our fear of God's grace, our passion to be self-sufficient, our unwillingness to accept God's forgiveness until we have earned it? Yes. I believe that one is much closer at hand. And the two are related.

I have come to believe that those financial problems are real. I believe they are much worse than we have been told. But I have also come to believe that the financial problem is probably caused by our lack of nerve, our fearing to face the spiritual dimension of our lives and of our society. The crisis of the churches is a call to us to become a community that celebrates the presence of God in the midst of life and the things of life.

I have come to see the answer not in bookkeeping and fund-raising, but in repentance and in a new, forgiving openness with one another and with God.

Guidelines for Endowed Congregations

1. Endowed congregations should be especially careful to make professional decisions about assets. They should be extremely careful to avoid placing congregation members in situations of conflict of interest. Each situation is unique, but these guidelines are suggested:

> a) Where possible, no one should serve on a board or committee making decisions that have direct financial consequences upon them or the institution that employs them.

> b) It is preferable in congregations for professional work to be clearly contracted for and paid for (audits, legal work, etc.).

2. Endowed congregations should all move as rapidly as possible toward having *annual certified audits*.

3. It should be clear in all fund management that the session (Board) of the congregation has final responsibility for all funds, regardless of how many separate funds there may be or how the session may set different guidelines for the different funds. No other legal entity should control the funds except under clear contract from the session (Board).

4. Where donors have wishes regarding the use of funds given to the congregation, it is the responsibility of the session (Board) to determine whether or not the purposes of the donor are consistent with the purposes of the congregation. If the session is not so satisfied, it should decline to receive the funds. If it is so satisfied, it is responsible to manage the funds in ways consistent with the donor's intent.

5. Endowed congregations should fulfill the denomination's requirements for financial disclosures. The congregations have a responsibility to clarify or improve the requirement where they feel it to be necessary.

6. All information about the endowment (income, expense, guidelines, etc.) should be available to any member of the congregation, and summaries should be widely available at congregation meetings, etc.

7. The session (Board) should see detailed reports from the fund trustees on a regular (suggested quarterly) basis. This should include a balance sheet. They should have opportunity to act on reports.

8. The fund trustees should receive and act on detailed reports more frequently (suggested monthly).

9. The public should have information if there is a need to know.

Caught in the Financial Bind: Reflections on Clergy and Money

(This is part of an article describing fourteen "binds" clergy experience in dealing with money. The full article appears in the July-August, 1996 issues of *Congregations*, published by the Alban Institute. These binds I personally experienced in the role of pastor.)

1. I understand my job as "pastor" to include being in a servant role, not "lording" it over others, and I often got in an emotional bind because I also wanted to have a salary based on my training and professional skills.

2. Leading the fall stewardship campaign was often uncomfortable for me. In a sense I kept being aware that I was asking people to contribute to my salary, which usually was the biggest item in the budget. Emotionally the bind had to do with asking people to pledge to God, but knowing it was coming to me.

3. There is a lot of acceptance for clergy being poor managers of resources. It is actually more acceptable in the church to be a financial klutz than a wizard. I experienced a bind between wanting to be really good at finances and throwing up my hands and letting others do it.

4. I often felt guilty about our family situation, aware that my children were paying fairly substantially because of my professional choices. I saw my kids having less than their friends, many from the congregation.

5. I believed in and practiced proportional giving/tithing, but couldn't get over feelings of resentment toward people of means who gave little in comparison with what seemed to be their resources.

6. At times friends/family members indicated to me that I would be better off if I would be more assertive and demand a better salary. I resented their saying that, and I also resented my own inability to be assertive.

7. As pastor I was often aware of pressing financial needs of some members of the congregation, and that awareness made me a poor advocate for my own needs.

8. When my spouse's salary became necessary to handle our family's needs, all of the above binds got tighter, and there was less and less time to deal with it all.

9. There is a feeling in the church (obviously at least partially internalized by many of us) that inadequate salaries are virtuous. The opportunity to do the work ought to be reward enough.

10. Clergy often feel a need to raise questions about the materialistic assumptions of society at the same time they have a voice inside crying out for more of the fruits of that materialism for themselves.

11. Clergy often find themselves in a bind in listening to the biblical advice to take no care for the future at the same time that they are worrying about pension payment.

12. Clergy often are expected to participate in the lives of laity whose activities include being in clubs or situations clergy cannot afford.

13. Clergy often feel patronized by people who want to pass along to them their leftovers of clothing or furniture. The hard part is saying "thank you," especially when you are choked up with anger.

14. Clergy are highly aware of the differential in salary among them. They find all kinds of emotional binds—resentment, bitterness—which poison relationships among clergy and make collegiality difficult.

Please note: This is a confessional list. I am not at all proud of experiencing most of these "binds" and the feelings lying behind them. I share them here to help clergy look at the binds in their own lives and to help laypeople recognize and empathize with some clergy issues. I hope some who read this book will make it an occasion for opening up such feelings to one another.

NOTES

Chapter 1

1. See the analysis accompanying data presented in a series of annual publications: John Ronsvalle and Sylvia Ronsvalle, *The State of Church Giving* (Champaign, Ill.: empty tomb, inc.), especially 1993, 84-86.

2. I have been a life-long partisan of congregations, and I expect my readers have a strong commitment also. In this book I make no defense of why congregational life is important or *why* I am concerned about the impact of congregational meltdown. For those looking for such a defense of congregations, I recommend: Nancy Tatom Ammerman, *Congregation and Community* (New Brunswick, N.J.: Rutgers University Press, 1997).

3. Robert Wuthnow, *Crisis in the Churches: Spiritual Malaise, Fiscal Woe* (New York: Oxford University Press, 1997) explains at length the way clergy and laity today struggle with these issues.

Chapter 2

1. Dean Hoge, Jackson Carroll, and Francis Scheets, *Patterns of Parish Leadership: Costs and Effectiveness in Four Denominations* (Kansas City, Mo.: Sheed and Ward, 1988). The book addresses a number of questions about local congregations in Catholic, Episcopal, Evangelical Lutheran Church in America, and United Methodist denominations.

2. See Charles G. Campbell, "Creative Endowments" (doctoral dissertation, Hartford Seminary, 1991), for a dramatic case related to this

concern. He describes a careful effort to understand and manage an endowment of $517,000 given to South Congregational Church in Granby, Connecticut, in 1956. The congregation takes considerable pride in a number of far-reaching projects it supported with the endowment fund (intended to be "in perpetuity") between 1956 and 1990; such projects had cost $1,200,000, and the principal in 1990 was still $540,000. The dissertation deals with the history of the endowment, but also with the dramatic realization of what had happened while the church had "lived with" its endowment. They discovered that if they had simply placed the original gift in a savings account, it would have reached a value of $3,855,171 by 1990. In effect, while feeling good about how the endowment was being spent, they had permitted a major resource to evaporate $2,000,000 of its ability to support their mission.

3. A recent headline about the Assemblies of God read: "Layoffs Avoided in Downsizing." And yet the text did admit that "The officially termed 'reengineering program' began in 1994 and has resulted in a 10 percent work-force reduction of seventy-five employees." See "Layoffs Avoided in Downsizing," *Christianity Today,* 7 April 1997, 51.

4. Robert Wilson and Paul Mickey, *What New Creation: The Agony of Church Restructure* (Nashville: Abingdon Press, 1977). The pioneers' questions about restructuring are as relevant today as they were in the mid 70s as they wrote about changes of the late 60s and early 70s. The description they write about the state of denominational offices and the role of the national denominational staff persons in those days 30 years ago would be a fair picture of much of the tension in those offices and staff persons today.

5. *News Briefs: Presbyterian Church (USA),* 12 May 1995; 9 June 1995.

6. *National Catholic Reporter,* 30 September 1994.

7. "A Church in Crisis Over Arts," *New York Times,* 2 May 1995, A-16.

8. See Loren Mead, *Five Challenges for the Once and Future Church* (Bethesda, Md.: the Alban Institute, 1996). I deal with this issue at some length here, especially in ch. 2.

9. Claude A. Smith, "Ordained Ministry and Its Financing: A Report with Critical Commentary," July 1996. An Episcopal clergyman, Smith did his paper through a grant from Lilly Endowment, Inc.

10. In this case Smith's percentage is of only 5,718 congregations in that denomination from which he could gather data.

11. See also Loren Mead, *Transforming Congregations for the Future* (Bethesda, Md.: the Alban Institute, 1994), 14-15.

12. "Survey Data from 85 Congregations in the Episcopal Diocese of Massachusetts for 1994-95." Used by permission.

13. Kenneth Bedell, ed., *Yearbook of American and Canadian Churches* (Nashville: Abingdon Press).

14. Roger Finke and Rodney Stark, *The Churching of America, 1776-1990: Winners and Losers in Our Religious Economy* (New Brunswick, N.J.: Rutgers University Press, 1994), makes a case for a two-century pattern of steady growth among the evangelical, conservative religious bodies and a decline in the more establishment, mainline churches.

15. David A. Roozen and Jackson W. Carroll, "Recent Trends in Church Membership Participation," in *Understanding Church Growth and Decline,* Dean R. Hoge and David A. Roozen, eds. (New York: Pilgrim Press, 1979), 39-40.

16. See Loren Mead, *The Once and Future Church* (Bethesda, Md.: the Alban Institute, 1991), where this is discussed in terms of the current paradigm shift.

17. John Ronsvalle and Sylvia Ronsvalle, *The State of Church Giving Through 1993* (Champaign, Ill.: the empty tomb, inc.), 79-97. They return to their United Theory of Giving and Membership in their 1994 volume.

18. The Ronsvalles' annual *State of Church Giving* reports have been most helpful, although many sociologists and church executives argue with their methods and conclusions. See also John Ronsvalle and Sylvia Ronsvalle, *Behind the Stained Glass Windows: Money Dynamics in the Church* (Grand Rapids: Baker, 1996). Dean Hoge, Charles Zech, Patrick McNamara, and Michael Donahue, *Money Matters: Personal Giving in American Churches* (Louisville: Westminster John Knox Press, 1996), a substantial study of how giving is thought about and carried out in congregations of five denominations. Joseph Claude Harris, *The Cost of Catholic Parishes and Schools* (Kansas City, Mo.: Sheed and Ward, 1996). Robert Wuthnow, *The Crisis in the Churches: Spiritual Malaise, Fiscal Woe* (New York: Oxford University Press, 1997), explores the great difficulty religious leaders have approaching the issues of money, giving, and God. Also a number of papers are currently being written and new books are on the way.

19. Ronsvalle and Ronsvalle, *The State of Church Giving Through 1994.*

20. Ibid.

21. Hoge, Zech, McNamara, and Donahue, *Money Matters,* 63.

Chapter 3

1. See Loren Mead, *Transforming Congregations for the Future* (Bethesda, Md.: the Alban Institute, 1994), ch. 1, 5, where I began working on some of these matters. Friends and critics have suggested substantial additions and changes to that material, and I hope I do them justice here. Obviously we have just scratched the surface; it seems to make us very nervous to talk about such subjects.

2. The information on this chart is provided from a public report of the General Council on Finance and Administration of the United Methodist Church in the United States of America. It lists the amounts of expenditures from each dollar received for the period from 1973 to 1994, adjusting the 1973 totals to eliminate the effects of inflation as measured by the Consumer Price Index. Used by permission.

3. John Ronsvalle and Sylvia Ronsvalle, *The State of Church Giving through 1994* (Champaign, Ill.: empty tomb, inc., 1996).

4. Personal correspondence, 16 November 1993.

5. Personal correspondence, 18 September 1996.

6. *The Reluctant Steward: A Report and Commentary* (Indianapolis: Christian Theological Seminary and St. Meinrad's Seminary, 1992). This brief but penetrating study led by David Conway makes clear the fact that pastors and seminary students have little interest in financial management or in learning about it. With clergy demonstrating this attitude, one need not wonder why a strong sense of fiduciary trusteeship has been allowed to erode. I say more about this interesting issue in chapter 7.

7. *Report of the President, 1995.* This statement was published by the Evangelical Lutheran Church in America for use that year in the Synod Assemblies.

8. See "Board of Pensions Nervously Eyes Rising Health-Care Costs," *News Briefs* (Presbyterian News Service), 25 July 1997. Across the denominations, "nervous eyes" are cast in the same direction, with real cause.

9. I have been surprised by the depth of lay resentment toward this "perk" as some see it. The resentment seems to stem from an attitude of *I have to buy my house out of my salary, and I don't get a tax break. Why should the pastor get special treatment?* Unfortunately the resentment is often directed at clergy by congregations and even church boards. I feel that anger about a governmental policy is displaced upon the person who does not make the policy but simply benefits from it. This is anger from which clergy find it hard to extricate themselves.

10. The scenario is not entirely absurd. While I was president of the Alban Institute, we ran into an interesting problem when we tried to organize the least expensive training program for pastors—right after Christmas. We discovered that the cheapest place to have such a conference was the Bahamas. We found clergy wouldn't sign up. They apparently were unwilling to try to tell their boards that they wanted to spend their continuing education funds in the Bahamas in January, though we couldn't find a cheaper appropriate place. We never tried it again.

11. For more discussion of this issue see Loren Mead, *The Once and Future Church* (Bethesda, Md.: the Alban Institute, 1991). See also Mead, *Transforming Congregations for the Future*, 87-89.

12. Diane Winston, "Dollars and Sense," *Dallas Morning News,* 17 August 1996.

13. Again, please note that I am not equating these as equally "bad," deplorable, or damaging. I am saying that our unwillingness to go public with the problem and our unwillingness to act seriously on it is uncomfortably reminiscent of how we dealt with sexual abuse for all too many years.

14. My dentist, a United Methodist, told me of his surprise to discover that his local church was involved in six lawsuits in one year: people slipping on icy sidewalks, a child falling off playground equipment, and the like.

Chapter 4

1. I claim some seniority on this one. My grandfather's telephone number in Gloucester, Massachusetts, was 1. That's all, just 1. My father's office was 24. Home was 367, which for years–until they changed the Episcopal hymnbook—was always a favorite hymn. My congregation wondered why I picked it so often.

2. There were some small areas in which local phone companies were exclusive local suppliers.

3. I lean heavily on the studies of Robert Wood Lynn, former vice president of Lilly Endowment, Inc. A gifted church historian, Lynn's studies of the financing of religious institutions will, when published, alert us to the remarkable innovation with which church leaders have faced the financing of their institutions. Lynn's studies undergird a number of addresses he has given to church leaders. They will be reported in a book to be published by the Alban Institute in 1998.

4. Stephen F. Hopkins, a staff member of the Anglican Diocese of Niagara, has written a paper with a catchy title: "Resurrection, Resuscitation, or Taxidermy?" I fear we are tempted to try the latter two. Hopkins explores the Canadian religious scene.

5. Another automobile example was the most dramatic expression of this managerial elite—the invention and marketing of the disastrous Edsel.

6. I am fully aware of the inadequacy of this language to the theological truth that the church exists for those outside its life. In that sense, the "customer," not the church member, is the recipient of the church's care. But here I am violating that theological point to make another. Try to stay with me and see where I am going.

7. I know this language may be offensive. I do not mean it as an offense but as a way to throw a different perspective on our familiar institutional forms. Churches mean much more to me than any "industry." Yet I use the word to describe the church, so as to capture an aspect of church life that we do not often look at. Forgive me if you find the word offensive. In a way, I do, too.

8. Hopkins, "Resurrection, Resuscitation, or Taxidermy?"

Chapter 5

1. To admit my personal prejudice, this is the standard of giving that I learned from my father. Despite its faults, it is the standard my wife and I have long preferred. We are not very precise and legalistic about it, but it is 10 percent and it comes off the top. We do not give it all to the local church.

2. Not much has been written about endowments in congregations.

Within both the Presbyterian and Episcopal Churches, however, groups of congregations do meet annually to discuss how to be better managers and users of their endowments. The Alban Institute has several short research papers on its on-demand publications list that deal with endowments in congregations.

3. A friend once told me that church people, like university people, want the money that supports their work to come in over the transom. At night. They don't want to have to deal with it otherwise. I'm not sure he was exaggerating.

4. "Profits at the Altar," *Fortune,* 9 September 1996, 120-26, notes the formation of the Revelation Corporation, which intends to help some congregations by building a marketing network among eighteen million church members, returning some of the profits from sales of merchandise, insurance, mortgages, and other commodities to the congregations whose members do the purchasing. This is pushing fund raising further than my comfort level, but those congregations have found it a challenging direction.

5. As with tithing, I am poking at something I believe in and try to practice. But functionally the word is used in such a way that it does not accomplish what we intend it to. Its meaning seems to vary, depending on who uses and hears it.

Chapter 6

1. Loren Mead, *The Once and Future Church* (Bethesda, Md.: the Alban Institute, 1991); *Transforming Congregations for the Future* (Bethesda, Md.: the Alban Institute, 1994); *Five Challenges for the Once and Future Church* (Bethesda, Md.: the Alban Institute, 1996). These three books are related to one another, as described in *Five Chal-lenges.* Each builds on the previous, although they were not planned as a continuous presentation. They represent a trail I have been following, trying to understand what is happening in the churches with which I am familiar. The current book stands by itself, though the trail blazed in the previous books led me to the unacknowledged issue of money.

2. As a friend says, "We are like a rich man whose income comes from an oil field that has only twenty years of productive life ahead of it."

3. I recommend the following kit that includes board game, videotape, and parents' guide: Nathan Dungan, *Parents, Kids, and Money.*

Available from the Lutheran Brotherhood, 625 Fourth Ave. S., Minneapolis, Minn. 55415.

4. Ministry of Money, 2 Professional Drive, Suite 220, Gaithersburg, Md. 20897. I have participated in several Ministry of Money seminars and have been helped by them. I don't know anyone else who has even tried to go as far in addressing this concern.

See also Jacob Needleman, *Money and the Meaning of Life* (New York: Doubleday, 1991).

5. Allen Farnham, "The Windfall Awaiting the New Inheritors," *Fortune*, May 1990, let the cat out of the bag. He noted that in the next decade or so an incredible amount of wealth would be transferred from one generation to another through bequests. That concept of windfall has echoed through the development office of every nonprofit in the country. The article has been updated and the numbers changed regularly ever since. Interestingly enough, the most recent I've seen is an article by my own son, Walter Russell Mead, "Outrageous Fortune," *The American Benefactor,* Spring 1997, 68-72.

6. Clergy, I hope you know I am one of you, and I claim you as my brothers and sisters. But this is one place where I have to speak the truth to you as a group. I know there are exceptions—praise God. Try to hear this as a message from one who loves and believes in you.

7. Dean Hoge, Charles Zech, Patrick McNamara, and Michael Donahue in *Money Matters* (Louisville: Westminster John Knox, 1996) give more complex descriptions than I do here. Different denominations do have different approaches to fund-raising. I am oversimplifying.

8. Addresses: Consortium of Endowed Episcopal Congregations, Box 183, Pennington, N.J. 08534-0183. The National Association of Endowed Presbyterian Churches, 807 West 32nd St., Wilmington, Del. 19802. The Presbyterian network has available a 1995 survey of 142 churches with endowments. Churches were surveyed by mail to discover "how endowed Presbyterian churches manage, utilize, view, and grow their invested funds."

Chapter 7

1. Some of the ideas in this chapter first appeared in Loren Mead, "Wealth and Stewardship: An Interactive Exploration of Law and Grace," *The Journal of Stewardship,* 49 (1997): 35-40.

Appendix A

1. This set of guidelines was developed in a workshop at the annual meeting of the Network of Endowed Presbyterian Congregations, meeting in Washington on September 9, 1988. This report is reprinted from *Action Information* for January-February, 1988, 9.

BIBLIOGRAPHY

There are dozens, perhaps hundreds of books about stewardship and money. These are the ones I found particularly helpful in trying to understand what is happening. Among the philosophical or theological works, I choose only one, by Needleman.

Conway, David. *The Reluctant Steward.* Indianapolis: Christian Theological Seminar and St. Meinrad's Seminary, 1992.

Harris, Joseph Claude. *The Cost of Catholic Parishes and Schools.* Kansas City, Mo.: Sheed and Ward, 1996.

Hoge, Dean R., Jackson W. Carroll, and Francis K. Scheets. *Patterns of Parish Leadership.* Kansas City, Mo.: Sheed and Ward, 1988.

Hoge, Dean R., Charles E. Zech, Patrick McNamara, and Michael Donahue. *Money Matters: Personal Giving in American Churches.* Louisville: Westminster John Knox Press, 1996.

Mickey, Paul, and Robert Wilson. *What New Creation?* Nashville: Abingdon Press, 1977.

Needleman, Jacob. *Money and the Meaning of Life.* New York: Doubleday, 1991.

Ronsvalle, John, and Sylvia Ronsvalle. *Behind the Stained Glass Windows: Money Dynamics in the Church.* Grand Rapids: Baker Books, 1996.

————. *The State of Church Giving through 1993, 1994.* Champaign, Ill.: empty tomb, inc., 1996.

Schmidt, J. David. *Choosing to Live.* Milwaukee: Christian Steward-ship Association, 1996.

Vallet, Ronald E., and Charles E. Zech. *The Mainline Church's Funding Crisis: Issues and Possibilities.* Grand Rapids: Eerdmans, 1995.

Wuthnow, Robert. *God and Mammon in America.* New York: The Free Press, 1994.

————. *The Crisis of the Churches.* New York: Oxford, 1997.

————. *Poor Richard's Principle.* Princeton, N.J.: Princeton University Press, 1996.

————, ed. *Rethinking Materialism.* Grand Rapids: Eerdmans, 1995.